The
ESL
Miscellany

*A cultural and linguistic inventory
of American English*

Resource Handbook Number 2

by Raymond C. Clark, Patrick R. Moran, and Arthur A. Burrows

with a photographic study of American gestures
by Peg Clement

PRO LINGUA ASSOCIATES

Published by Pro Lingua Associates
Brattleboro, Vermont 05301

ISBN 0-86647-001-8

Library of Congress Cataloguing in Publication Data:

Moran, Patrick R.
    The ESL miscellany.

    (Resource handbook / Pro Lingua Associates ; no. 2)
    Bibliography: p.
    Includes index.
    1. English language--Study and teaching--Foreign students--Handbooks, manuals, etc. 2. English language --Text-books for foreigners. 3. English language-- United States. I. Clark, Raymond C., 1937-
II. Burrows, Arthur A., 1942-   . III. Clement, Peg.
IV. Title. V. Series: Resource handbook ; no. 2.
PE1128.A2M58   428.2'4'071073   81-8581
ISBN 0-86647-001-8   AACR2

Printed in the United States of America

Second printing, 1984

ACKNOWLEDGEMENTS

The first thing we should say is that a lot of people helped us and we appreciate their support. They have made the development of this book an enjoyable experience. Before we try to name and thank our helpers, however, the second thing we should say is that we assume the full responsibility for any errors or inaccuracies or failures of judgement that may occur in this book. In other words, don't blame them, blame us.

The idea for this book came out of a project initiated at the School for International Training in 1977 for the U.S. Peace Corps. A graduate student in the MAT program, Eleanor Boone, with assistance from Rick Gildea and with support and advice from Mike Jerald, Mary Clark and Ray Clark was contracted by Peace Corps to develop a manual of practical suggestions for Peace Corps volunteers teaching English as a foreign language. Toward the end of the project, Eleanor was joined by Pat Moran who, at Ray Clark's suggestion, compiled an appendix of information about the English language. The appendix was intended to be useful to the Peace Corps English teacher lost deep in the back-country with no professional library to speak of, and nowhere to turn for such things as punctuation guidelines and metric conversion charts.

Two years later, with the appendix in mind, Ray, Pat and Andy along with Mike Jerald, Peg Clement, Marilyn Funk and John Croes began developing additional resource materials that might be useful to the ESL teacher.

Pat's appendix has now become a book in its own right - a book that represents a collective effort by its three authors. The section on gestures however, is exclusively the work of Peg Clement who allowed us to use the photos from her MAT thesis (Peg in turn, would like to acknowledge the help of George McFadden who took the pictures, and Mike Jerald who processed them).

It should be obvious that a book such as this one is built upon the work and publications of many other people. We will not list them here, but we would like to call your attention to the list of sources at the back of the book. We have also mentioned sources in footnotes within the text itself wherever we have relied heavily and exclusively on information from one source.

And now to name our helpers. Susannah Clark spent many long hours in the Brooks Memorial Library producing the first draft of many of the Topics. She also took on the task of deciphering her father's handwriting and alphabetizing several of the other Topics.

Mary Clark suggested the title for our wild array of information. We think it's a good one. She also gave us permission to use and adapt her chart on modal verbs.

Diane Larsen-Freeman looked over the final draft of the Linguistic Aspect and made several suggestions that improved that section. Mike Jerald and Bonnie Mennell helped us out by reviewing our lists of topics. They added several words and raised several good questions. Marty Fleischer pointed out to us that our law topic didn't adequately cover crime and police work. So Topic #45 came into being.

Karen Kale not only agreed to review our list of Situations, she also did it on short notice and while she was packing for a trip to Denmark. She suggested Situation #7, Academia, to us - a good suggestion.

Marty Fleisher somehow managed to convert page after page of handwritten lists on all kinds of scrap papers into nicely typed pages. She also corrected spelling, added punctuation and added an occasional word here and there. Lisa Cook typed the last minute additions and corrections.

A few pages of the first draft that were handed to Marty were actually quite well typed, but Susan McBean did that.

And so we come back to ourselves for a final pat on the back. Pat contributed the illustrations. Andy designed the book and Ray tried to exercise editorial judgement where and when it was needed.

Finally, we would like to acknowledge The Experiment in International Living in Brattleboro for the use of its IBM OS-6 which we used to set the final copy of the manuscript.

TABLE OF CONTENTS

Topics

INTRODUCTION

The Purpose and Contents

of The Miscellany

This book is a compendium of useful and interesting information for the teacher and student of English as a Second Language. Although the book will be of greatest interest to teachers and students of American English, it will also be useful to teachers and students who are involved with other varieties of English.

The teacher will find this book helpful as a resource for developing material. Virtually every teacher at some time or another attempts to develop material of his/her own either to supplement a basic text, to expand upon some point, to replace or adapt inadequate material or develop a complete curriculum from scratch. This one book may not contain everything that the teacher/materials developer needs to know, but we believe it is the most comprehensive one-volume reference available to the lesson writer.

In addition to its usefulness in developing materials, this book offers another function: that of a guideline/checklist for the teacher who practices eclecticism. More and more teachers, rather than stick to one comprehensive program or one set method, find that in order to keep their classes relevant and interesting they find it necessary to teach "a little of this and a little of that." The problem with this kind of eclecticism, of course, is that it is not always easy to know if everything is being covered. This book, or for that matter any book, will not be able to tell you everything you need to know about American English, but it can serve as a comprehensive outline. By consulting the list of Situations, for example, the teacher can rather quickly get a sense for which conversational situations have been covered and what remains to be covered.

A third use for this book is that many of the lists can be used just as they are as hand-outs. For example, the one-page summary of religions in America could be copied and given to the students as the point of reference for a question-answer practice or discussion of religion in America. For that reason we encourage the copying of these lists for classroom use.

We suggested earlier that students of American English will also find this book useful, but it is likely that it will be especially valuable to advanced students of American English who are in need of a one-volume guide that will help them determine what they already know and what they should focus their study on. We think this book will be of particular interest to advanced students who are preparing to be teachers of English as a Second Language.

The Miscellany is divided into five parts. Parts I and II contain information about the language itself. This information is classified in two major aspects: Linguistic and Communicative. The linguistic aspect contains information that in some way deals with what is commonly called the grammar or structure of the language. However, this linguistic aspect is not a grammar, but rather a series of lists of words and forms that exemplify some grammar point. For example, under two-word verbs, there will be no rules for the use of two-word verbs. Instead, there will be a list of separable and inseparable two-word verbs. In other words, it is assumed that the user will have some understanding of how two-word verbs function in English.

The communicative aspect does not deal with linguistic forms such as "go, went, gone" but outlines ways in which the language is used to send and receive messages. We have included lists of functions such as asking, introducing, telling, etc. We have also included in the communicative aspect vocabulary lists that outline potential topics of conversations and we have compiled lists of situations in which communicative functions and topics of conversation are carried out.

To make all this information about the linguistic and communicative aspects of language more useful to the lesson planner, we have also provided a framework for lesson planning that will give the materials developer a way of bringing together in one lesson the what, how and where of language use.

In Part III we have compiled several lists that form an outline of American culture. Each list can be used as the basic data upon which can be based a discussion or controlled conversation about some facet of American culture. Part III can be used as the basis for an orientation to immigration and resettlement in the United States.

Part IV is a pot-pourri of information that is, in general, meta-linguistic. In other words, the information in this part will help the teacher and the learner facilitate the teaching/learning process. But there is also information that does not fit neatly into any of the other categories and is best labelled as miscellaneous.

Part V needs little explanation. It contains some examples of communicative systems that parallel the language itself. Hence, we have called it the paralinguistic aspect. Of greatest interest is a photographic catalog of almost 50 gestures that are commonly recognized and understood in the United States. We have provided titles for the gestures, but otherwise we leave it up to you, the user of this book, to discuss, compare, practice and even add to this listing.

We will be the first to admit that this volume represents an ambitious undertaking that probably contains inaccuracies, and that is far from complete. Furthermore, the nature of the information itself is such that it may need occasional up-dating. It is our hope and intention to eventually produce a revision, and to make the revised edition more useful and comprehensive, we ask you, the users, to help us in this effort with your suggestions. Send them to us at the address below and we will make every effort to use and acknowledge your contribution.

PRO LINGUA ASSOCIATES
15 Elm Street
Brattleboro, Vermont   05301

```
┌─────────────────────────────────────┐
│                                     │
│          The Lesson Plan            │
│                                     │
│       (A Word to the Teacher)       │
│                                     │
└─────────────────────────────────────┘
```

One approach to teaching an ESL lesson is to pose to yourself the basic question words:

WHAT am I going to teach, i.e. what is my subject matter: verbs? How to exchange greetings?

HOW am I going to teach it, i.e. which method, technique, procedure will I use?

WHO am I teaching, i.e. what are my students' needs, abilities, interests?

WHERE and WHEN am I teaching and how do these physical and temporal surroundings affect the lesson?

WHY am I teaching this lesson, i.e. can I easily state an objective for the lesson I have chosen to teach, and is that objective reasonable in light of the questions I have asked above?

Using these questions as a base, we can construct a simple framework that can serve as a lesson plan or a pre-lesson checklist to insure that our lesson will make sense.

But the WHAT of ESL is a very complicated thing, and needs elaboration. As language teachers we are involved in two WHATS: the medium and the message. We can consider that the medium is the grammar and the message is the thoughts, concepts, ideas, attitudes that are conveyed from one speaker to another. Then there is the culture in which our language is embedded. The culture can be considered as a kind of over-lay that sometimes affects the medium and most usually influences the message. If part of our purpose (WHY) is to enable our students to use the language in culturally appropriate and effective ways, then we must consider the cultural aspect of language teaching.

To provide a systematic approach to the WHAT of language teaching, the lesson plan/checklist is divided into three WHATS. WHAT #1 we call the linguistic aspect and is, for all intents and purposes, the grammar of the language. So on our plan/checklist an appropriate entry might be: Past tense of BE (35). This means that one of the purposes of our lesson is to work on WAS and WERE, and it happens to be step 35 along our grammatical sequence.

WHAT #2 we call the communicative aspect because it goes beyond linguistic forms such as WAS and WERE and deals with messages. Specifically, it includes the context of the message (SITUATION) or where and when the text of the lesson is to be used. This particular sub-aspect, the situation, is usually only relevant where we are dealing with communicative acts, i.e. dialogues, conversations, interviews, etc.

A second sub-aspect we have labelled as TOPIC, meaning the topic of the conversation, reading, drama, interview, etc. In other words, what subject is being discussed: the weather? sports? street directions?

The final communicative sub-aspect is called FUNCTION, and in many ways is strictly speaking more a matter of forms than content, but since content is necessarily present, we have included it here. The FUNCTIONS we have in mind are basically the functions of a national-functional syllabus and include communicative functions such as asking, telling, ordering, explaining, etc.

WHAT #3 is the cultural over-lay. It may be a significant part of the lesson, or it may be almost totally lacking. For example, if the topic is politics and if the students are preparing to use their English in the United States, then the peculiarities of the American political system will at least influence the vocabulary of our lesson, i.e. the TOPIC.

In our lesson plan/checklist we have included a line for HOW. A typical entry beside this item might be pattern practice, or dialogue, or perhaps both. Because this miscellany is not intended to be directly about pedagogy, we have not included any descriptions of teaching methods and techniques, but we would like to call your attention to our own publication, Language Teaching Techniques, in which we have described over two dozen basic teaching techniques.

Finally, the items marked OBJECTIVE and EVALUATION deal with the WHY of our lesson. Quite simply, the objective should state what we expect our students to be able to do at the end of the lesson that they couldn't do at the beginning, and the evaluation is our way of testing to see if in fact, when the lesson is over, we (teacher and students) have achieved the objective.

LESSON PLAN/CHECKLIST

BACKGROUND INFORMATION/NOTES:
    (WHO, WHERE, WHEN)

OBJECTIVE:
    (WHY)

LINGUISTIC ASPECT:
    (WHAT #1)

COMMUNICATIVE ASPECT:
    (WHAT #2)

        A. SITUATION:

        B. TOPIC:

        C. FUNCTION:

CULTURAL ASPECT:
    (WHAT #3)

PEDAGOGY:
    (HOW)

EVALUATION:

The Learning Plan

(A Word to the Student)

You can use this book in many ways. Here is one way. Look at each section in this book to see what you know and don't know. Then ask yourself do I need to know? Use the outline below to help make your learning plan. In each square write in the numbers. For example, if you know most everything in Grammar List 1, write G1 under I know.

	I know	I don't know	I need to know
Grammar Lists G1-22			
Situations S1-10			

	I know	I don't know	I need to know
Topics T1-53			
Functions F1-4			
Cultural Lists C1-31			
Metalinguistic & Miscellaneous Lists M1-14			
Paralinguistic P1-4			

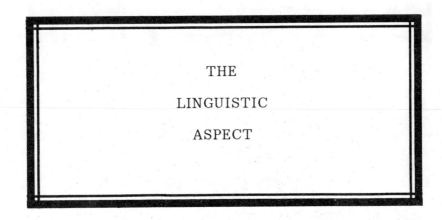

THE

LINGUISTIC

ASPECT

For years, the teaching and learning of English has focused on texts, techniques and exercises designed to enable students to manipulate the grammar of English with a minimum of grammatical errors such as 'he go' and with clear pronunciation. Obviously, this is still an important part of the teaching of English; there will always be a time and place for the tried and true exercises and drills that help instill grammatical accuracy. Practice still makes perfect.

On the following pages we have provided first a checklist of grammatical features that most teachers find it necessary to cover. This checklist is not intended to represent the best pedagogical sequence of what should be taught before what; it is only one possible sequence in which English grammar can be presented.

After the checklist are several selected lists that should prove helpful to the teacher or student who wants to work on a particular grammatical problem. It should be obvious that many syntactic features do not lend themselves to listing and so they will not be represented in the lists.

A Grammatical Sequence

The grammatical sequence on the following pages is to be considered only a handy check-list for the person who wants to get a rough idea of what can or should be covered in an English course. We make no claims that it is complete or logical or carefully programmed in steps of equal difficulty or complexity. We have listed 139 steps and we have placed them in a particular order. Some of the steps are big and some are small. Some steps can be omitted or placed elsewhere in the sequence, and some depend upon previous steps and should only be re-arranged with care. It will also be obvious that in some cases, two or more steps must be taken at the same time. In other words, please use this sequence with the understanding that it is not a grammar of English and it is not THE best or THE most natural sequence for proceeding through a grammatically-based English course.

The sequence does represent an attempt to proceed one step at a time through the grammar of English in a general progression of "easy and simple" points to "difficult and complex" points. It also represents a sequence that begins with useful and necessary points and leads to less useful and less necessary points. At the very least, the sequence represents dozens of potential grammar lessons that nearly every teacher and student will need to struggle with in a basic English program. Mastery of what this sequence represents, along with commensurate progress in pronunciation and communicative skills, would probably mean that the student is capable of functioning independently in an English-speaking world.

1. ___ Statement word order with BE.   I am here.

2. ___ Forms of BE.   Am; are; is.

3. ___ Subject pronouns.   I, you, he, she, it, we, they

4. ___ Question word order with BE.   Is he here?

5. ___ Negative of BE.   I am not; you are not

6. ___ Plural of regular Nouns.   We are students.

7. ___ Common irregular noun plurals.   They are women.

8. ___ Nationality words.   I am Swedish.
They are Swedish.

9. ___ Indefinite article: A/AN   I am an American.

10. ___	Question word: WHO	Who is she?
11. ___	AND in compound sentences.	He is a teacher and she is a student.
12. ___	BUT in compound sentences.	He is a teacher but she is not.
13. ___	Contractions of BE and NOT.	I'm not; he isn't.
14. ___	Conjugation of verbs other than BE. (3rd person-S)	I teach French. She teaches English.
15. ___	Questions and negatives with verbs using DO.	Do you speak.......? I don't speak.......?
16. ___	HAVE and HAVE GOT	I have....; I have got...
17. ___	Contractions of HAVE	I've.... I've got...
18. ___	Question word: WHAT	What do you have?
19. ___	Short answers.	Yes I do. No he isn't.
20. ___	Tag questions	You have....., don't you? You don't have.., do you?
21. ___	Negative questions	Don't you have......?
22. ___	Stative verbs	I want.....
23. ___	Positive imperative	Take a ......
24. ___	Negative imperative	Don't take a .....
25. ___	Colors	Take a red ....
26. ___	Definite and indefinite articles	...a yellow pencil; ...the yellow pencil
27. ___	Polite requests: WOULD, WILL COULD, WHY DON'T YOU	Would you......
28. ___	Demonstratives: THIS/THAT, THESE/THOSE	This is a ......
29. ___	Count and Non-count nouns.	This is soup. This is a spoon.
30. ___	Expletive THERE IS/ARE.	There's a fly....
31. ___	Expletive HERE	Here's a .....

32. ___	Expletive IT	It's cold.
33. ___	Form and position of modifiers	....green shoes
34. ___	Order of modifiers	..small green tennis shoes
35. ___	Past tense of BE.	I was .....
36. ___	Past tense of regular verbs	I studied ......
37. ___	Use of DID	Did you ...? No, I didn't ......
38. ___	Irregular past tense forms	I taught ......
39. ___	Question words as interrogative adjectives: WHAT, WHICH	Which book.....?
40. ___	SOME, ANY and NONE	I don't have any.....
41. ___	Quantity expressions (HOW) MUCH/MANY, FEW, LITTLE	I have a few......
42. ___	Use of QUITE and ONLY	I have quite a few...
43. ___	ONE as a pronoun	....the green one
44. ___	ONE OF/NONE OF	He needs one of the....
45. ___	THE OTHER/ANOTHER	She likes the other...
46. ___	EACH/EVERY/ALL OF	Each student has....
47. ___	Object pronouns	....understand her
48. ___	Direct and indirect objects	....give it to her
49. ___	Adverbs of frequency	He always ......
50. ___	EVER	Do you ever.....?
51. ___	Question words: HOW OFTEN, WHEN, WHERE	How often do you ....
52. ___	Cardinal and ordinal numbers	The first five ....
53. ___	Word order with place and time adverbials	... here in the morning.
54. ___	Prepositions with time expressions	... at three o'clock on Monday

55.	___	Prepositions with places	... on Main Street; in Brattleboro
56.	___	DO vs. MAKE	Do the dishes and make the bed
57.	___	Form and position of adverbs of manner (-LY)	... speak slowly
58.	___	Irregular adverbs of manner	... talk fast
59.	___	Question word: HOW	How does she ....?
60.	___	SAY, TELL, TALK, SPEAK	Tell me about ....
61.	___	Indirect object after ASK	Ask her a question.
62.	___	Indirect object with TO	Explain it to her.
63.	___	Indirect object with FOR	Do it for me.
64.	___	Present progressive (continuous)	I am _____ing.
65.	___	GOING TO future	I am going to _____.
66.	___	Question word: WHY	Why are you .....?
67.	___	Question word: WHAT....FOR	What are you ..... for?
68.	___	Question word: HOW COME...	How come you ...?
69.	___	Anticipatory IT	It's easy to ....
70.	___	LET'S	Let's .../ Let's not ...
71.	___	Idioms with GO	Let's go swimming.
72.	___	Indefinite YOU	You can't go swimming there.
73.	___	Question words: WHO vs. WHO(M)	Who sees Mary/whom does Mary see?
74.	___	Question word: WHOSE	Whose .... is this?
75.	___	Possessive Adjectives	That's my .....
76.	___	Possessive 'S	Mary's ... is here.
77.	___	Possessive OF	The leg of the table.
78.	___	Possessive pronouns	That's mine.

79. ___	BELONGS TO	That belongs to ....
80. ___	BE ABOUT TO future	I am about to ....
81. ___	Present tense for future time	I am to .... next week.
82. ___	Modals: CAN, MIGHT, SHOULD, MUST	We can go .....
83. ___	Modals: OUGHT TO	We ought to go ...
84. ___	HAVE TO	We have to go .....
85. ___	Modals in past tense with perfect aspect.	We could have gone. We had to go.
86. ___	Future tense with WILL	We'll go .....
87. ___	Contractions of WILL NOT	We won't go .....
88. ___	Future progressive	We will be going
89. ___	HAD BETTER	We'd better go....
90. ___	WOULD RATHER	I'd rather be a .....
91. ___	WOULD LIKE	I'd like to be a .....
92. ___	WAS GOING TO .... BUT	I was going to ... but
93. ___	AND ... TOO/EITHER	And she does too/And I won't either.
94. ___	Separable and inseparable two-word verbs	Let's call on them/Let's call them up.
95. ___	Adverbials of purpose: FOR and (IN ORDER) TO	He went for some books/ to buy some books.
96. ___	Adverbials of means and instrument: BY and WITH	He went by bus. He went with a suitcase.
97. ___	Verbs followed by an infinitive	I want to go.
98. ___	Verbs followed by a gerund	I enjoy singing.
99. ___	Verbs followed by an infinitive or a gerund	I like reading/to read.
100. ___	Perception verbs followed by simple verb instead of -ING.	I saw him go.

101. ___ VERY, TOO, ENOUGH   That's too big.

102. ___ Comparison: SAME AS,
    DIFFERENT FROM and LIKE This is the same as that.

103. ___ Comparison: THE SAME ____ Mine is the same color
    AS, AS _____ AS   as yours.

104. ___ Comparison: -ER THAN, It's bigger than his and
    MORE .... THAN   more useful than hers.

105. ___ Superlative   It's the biggest and the
            most useful.

106. ___ Past habitual   I used to ....

107. ___ WOULD as past habitual When we were young
            we would ....

108. ___ BE USED TO   I'm used to .....

109. ___ Causatives: LET, HAVE,
    HELP, MAKE and GET We made him go.

110. ___ Reflexive pronouns   He hurt himself.

111. ___ Emphatics   He did it himself.
            He himself did it.

112. ___ Embedded statements I know (that) he's here.

113. ___ Embedded question-word
    statements   I know where he is.

114. ___ Relative clauses   I know the man who did
            it.

115. ___ WHO/WHATEVER Whoever has ......

116. ___ FOR vs. DURING   ... during the afternoon
            for an hour

117. ___ Past continuous   He was studying ....

118. ___ WHILE and WHEN in clauses .... while I was sleeping

119. ___ BEFORE, UNTIL and AFTER He studied before you
            arrived.

120. ___ Present perfect   I have already studied.

121. ___ Irregular past participles She has gone.

122. ___	Participles as modifiers	He is boring/bored.
123. ___	STILL, ANYMORE, ALREADY YET	He hasn't studied yet.
124. ___	Present perfect progressive	They have been playing..
125. ___	Past perfect	They had gone
126. ___	Reported speech	He said she had gone.
127. ___	Past perfect progressive	They had been working ..
128. ___	Passive voice	They were seen by ....
129. ___	Adjective-preposition combinations	She is interested in ...
130. ___	Subjunctive	I suggested that she see ....
131. ___	WISH followed by noun clause	I wish (that) you were here.
132. ___	WISH and noun clause in past time	I wish (that) you had been here.
133. ___	Conditionals	If you were here .....
134. ___	Subordinators: UNLESS, BECAUSE, ALTHOUGH, WHETHER, WHENEVER	Unless I am mistaken ...
135. ___	Future perfect	They will have gone ....
136. ___	Future perfect progressive	They will have been working ....
137. ___	SO ... THAT vs. SUCH ... THAT	He is so strong that ....
138. ___	Nouns as complements	We elected him president.
139. ___	Verb-preposition combinations	We agreed on that.

Grammar Lists

Grammar Checklist

List #1: Minimal Pairs

Vowels*

/iy/	/i/
sheep	ship
leave	live
seat	sit
green	grin

/iy/	/ey/
eat	ate
see	say
week	wake
creep	crepe

/iy/	/e/
meet	met
mean	men
seeks	sex
beast	best

/i/	/ey/
it	ate
kick	cake
chin	chain
give	gave

/i/	/e/
pick	peck
did	dead
sit	set
knit	net

/i/	/æ/
big	bag
it	at
sit	sat
zig	zag

/i/	/ə/
big	bug
live	love
sick	suck
rib	rub

/ey/	/e/
wait	wet
date	debt
pain	pen

/ey/	/æ/
snake	snack
ate	at
made	mad
hate	hat

/ey/	/ə/
ape	up
lake	luck
rain	run
came	come

/ey/	/ow/
taste	toast
say	so
break	broke
wake	woke

/e/	/æ/
dead	dad
said	sad
men	man
bed	bad

/e/	/ə/
beg	bug
ten	ton
many	money
net	nut

/e/	/a/
get	got
step	stop
red	rod
net	not

/æ/	/ə/
grab	grub
swam	swum
mad	mud
cap	cup

*Trager-Smith System

Vowels (cont'd)

/æ/	/ɑ/
an	on
map	mop
cat	cot
lack	lock

/æ/	/ay/
am	I'm
sad	side
dad	died
back	bike

/ə/	/ɑ/
hug	hog
cup	cop
luck	lock
nut	not

/ə/	/u/
luck	look
buck	book
stud	stood
tuck	took

/ə/	/ow/
cut	coat
must	most
come	comb
but	boat

/ə/	/ɔ/
gun	gone
cut	caught
bus	boss
dug	dog

/ɑ/	/u/
lock	look
pot	put
cod	could
shock	shook

/ɑ/	/ow/
hop	hope
got	goat
want	won't
rod	road

/ɑ/	/ɔ/
cot	caught
sod	sawed
are	or
tock	talk

/ɑ/	/aw/
are	hour
shot	shout
dot	doubt
got	gout

/ɔ/	/oy/
all	oil
jaw	joy
ball	boil
bald	boiled

/u/	/uw/
full	fool
pull	pool
soot	suit
could	cooed

/u/	/ow/
bull	bowl
cook	coke
should	showed
brook	broke

/ow/	/oy/
toe	toy
old	oiled
bold	boiled
cone	coin

/aw/	/ay/
mouse	mice
tower	tire
proud	pride
found	find

/aw/	/oy/
owl	oil
vowed	void
sow	soy
bough	boy

/oy/	/ay/
toy	tie
boy	buy
voice	vice
alloy	ally

Consonants

/ p /   / b /

pig	big
cap	cab
pie	buy
rapid	rabid

/ b /   / v /

boat	vote
best	vest
curb	curve
cup-	covered
board	

/ l /   / r /

light	right
bowl	boar
collect	correct
lead	read

/ č /   / š /

cheap	sheep
catch	cash
watch	wash
cheese	she's

/ ĵ /   / š /

jeep	sheep
jade	shade
jack	shack
gyp	ship

/ ĵ /   / č /

gin	chin
joke	choke
jeer	cheer
junk	chunk

/ ĵ /   / y /

juice	use
jet	yet
jam	yam
wage	weigh

/ g /   / k /

bag	back
grape	crepe
glass	class
gap	cap

/ θ /   / t /

death	debt
thigh	tie
thin	tin
three	tree

/ θ /   / s /

think	sink
thing	sing
mouth	mouse
thin	sin

/ ð /   / d /

they	day
lather	ladder
their	dare
breathe	breed

List #2: Irregular Noun Plurals (7)*

A. Vowel change
man, men
woman, women
foot, feet
tooth, teeth
goose, geese
mouse, mice

B. -en Suffix
child, children
ox, oxen

C. f → v
thief, thieves
wife, wives
life, lives
knife, knives
calf, calves
half, halves
leaf, leaves
loaf, loaves
sheaf, sheaves
shelf, shelves
wolf, wolves
hoof, hooves

D. Same
sheep, sheep
deer, deer
moose, moose
fish, fish
trout, trout
salmon, salmon
bass, bass
series, series
means, means
species, species
Chinese, Chinese
Japanese, Japanese
Swiss, Swiss

E. No singular
scissors
tweezers
tongs
trousers
slacks
shorts
pants
pajamas
glasses
spectacles
binoculars
clothes
people

F. Foreign words
analysis, analyses
basis, bases
hypothesis, hypotheses
parenthesis, parentheses
synopsis, synopses
thesis, theses
crisis, crises

stimulus, stimuli
nucleus, nuclei
alumnus, alumni
radius, radii
syllabus, syllabi

medium, media
memorandum, memoranda
curriculum, curricula

phenomenon, phenomena
criterion, criteria

vortex, vortices
matrix, matrices
index, indices

---

*Number represents step in Grammatical Sequence (p. 10).

List #3: Nationality Words (8)*

Country	Person	Adjective
Afghanistan	Afghanistani	Afghan
		Afghani
Africa	African	African
Albania	Albanian	Albanian
Algeria	Algerian	Algerian
Andorra	Andorran	Andorran
Angola	Angolan	Angolan
Argentina	Argentinean	Argentinean
	Argentine	Argentine
Armenia	Armenian	Armenian
Asia	Asian	Asian
Australia	Australian	Australian
	Aussie (colloq.)	
Austria	Austrian	Austrian
Bahamas	Bahamian	Bahamian
Bahrain	Bahraini	Bahraini
Bangladesh	Bangladeshi	Bangladeshi
Belgium	Belgian	Belgian
Belize	Belizean	Belizean
Bhutan	Bhutanese	Bhutanese
	Bhutani	Bhutani
Bolivia	Bolivian	Bolivian
Brazil	Brazilian	Brazilian
Bulgaria	Bulgarian	Bulgarian
Burma	Burmese	Burmese
Cambodia (Kampuchea)	Cambodian	Cambodian
Cameroon	Cameroonian	Cameroonian
Canada	Canadian	Canadian
Cape Verde	Cape Verdean	Cape Verdean
Chad	Chadian	Chadian
Chile	Chilean	Chilean
Peoples Republic of China (Mainland China)	Chinese	Chinese
China (Taiwan)	Taiwanese	Taiwanese
Colombia	Colombian	Colombian
Congo	Congolese	Congolese
Costa Rica	Costa Rican	Costa Rican
Cuba	Cuban	Cuban
Cyprus	Cypriot	Cypriot
Czechoslovakia	Czech	Czech
	Czechoslovakian	

---

*Number represents step in Grammatical Sequence (p. 10).

Country	Person	Adjective
Denmark	Dane	Danish
Dominican Republic	Dominican	Dominican
Ecuador	Ecuadorian	Ecuadorian
Egypt	Egyptian	Egyptian
El Salvador	Salvadoran	Salvadoran
England	Englishman	English
Ethiopia	Ethiopian	Ethiopian
Europe	European	European
Fiji	Fiji Islander	Fijian
Finland	Finn	Finnish
France	Frenchman	French
Gabon	Gabonese	Gabonese
Gambia	Gambian	Gambian
German Democratic Republic	East German	East German
Germany (Federal Republic)	West German	West German
Ghana	Ghanaian	Ghanaian
Greece	Greek	Greek
Guatemala	Guatemalan	Guatemalan
Guinea	Guinean	Guinean
Guyana	Guyanese	Guyanese
Haiti	Haitian	Haitian
Honduras	Honduran	Honduran
Hungary	Hungarian	Hungarian
Iceland	Icelander	Icelandic
India	Indian	Indian
Indochina	Indochinese	Indochinese
Indonesia	Indonesian	Indonesian
Iran	Iranian	Iranian
Iraq	Iraqi	Iraqi
Ireland	Irishman	Irish
Israel	Israeli	Israeli
Italy	Italian	Italian
Ivory Coast	Ivorian	Ivorian
Jamaica	Jamaican	Jamaican
Japan	Japanese	Japanese
Jordan	Jordanian	Jordanian
Kampuchea (Cambodia)	Kampuchean	Kampuchean
Kenya	Kenyan	Kenyan
Korea, North	North Korean	North Korean
Korea, South	South Korean	South Korean
Kurdistan	Kurd	Kurdish
Kuwait	Kuwaiti	Kuwaiti

Country	Person	Adjective
Laos	Laotian	Laotian
Lebanon	Lebanese	Lebanese
Liberia	Liberian	Liberian
Libya	Libyan	Libyan
Malawi	Malawian	Malawian
Malaysia	Malaysian	Malaysian
Maldives	Maldivian	Maldivian
Mali	Malian	Malian
Malta	Maltese	Maltese
Mauritania	Mauritanian	Mauritanian
Mauritius	Mauritian	Mauritian
Mexico	Mexican	Mexican
Monaco	Monacan	Monacan
Mongolia	Mongolian	Mongolian
Morocco	Moroccan	Moroccan
Namibia	Namibian	Namibian
Nepal	Nepalese	Nepalese
Netherlands	Dutchman	Dutch
New Zealand	New Zealander	New Zealand
Nicaragua	Nicaraguan	Nicaraguan
Niger	Nigerien	Nigerien
Nigeria	Nigerian	Nigerian
Norway	Norwegian	Norwegian
Oman	Omani	Omani
Orient	Oriental	Oriental
Pakistan	Pakistani	Pakistani
Palestine	Palestinian	Palestinian
Panama	Panamanian	Panamanian
Paraguay	Paraguayan	Paraguayan
Peru	Peruvian	Peruvian
Philippines	Filipino	Filipino
Poland	Pole	Polish
Portugal	Portuguese	Portuguese
Puerto Rico	Puerto Rican	Puerto Rican
Romania	Romanian	Romanian
Saudia Arabia	Saudi	Saudi
		Saudi Arabian
Scotland	Scot; Scotsman	Scottish
Senegal	Senegalese	Senegalese
Solomon Islands	Solomon Islander	Solomon Island
Somalia	Somali	Somali
South Africa	South African	South African
Spain	Spaniard	Spanish
Sudan	Sudanese	Sudanese
Swaziland	Swazi	Swazi

Country	Person	Adjective
Sweden	Swede	Swedish
Switzerland	Swiss	Swiss
Syria	Syrian	Syrian
Tanzania	Tanzanian	Tanzanian
Thailand	Thai	Thai
Tibet	Tibetan	Tibetan
Togo	Togolese	Togolese
Tonga	Tongan	Tongan
Tunisia	Tunisian	Tunisian
Turkey	Turk	Turkish
Uganda	Ugandan	Ugandan
U.S.S.R.	Russian	Russian
		Soviet
United Kingdom	Briton	British
United States of America	American	American
Uruguay	Uruguayan	Uruguayan
Venezuela	Venezuelan	Venezuelan
Vietnam	Vietnamese	Vietnamese
Wales	Welshman	Welsh
Western Samoa	Samoan	Western Samoan
Yemen	Yemeni	Yemeni
Yemen, P.D.R.	South Yemeni	South Yemeni
Yugoslavia	Yugoslav	Yugoslav
Zaire	Zairian	Zairian
Zambia	Zambian	Zambian
Zimbabwe	Zimbabwean	Zimbabwean

A prize to anyone who provides us with proven, commonly-accepted terms for the following nations: Benin, Botswana, Burundi, Central African Republic, Guinea-Bissau, Liechtenstein, Luxembourg, Madagascar, Mozambique, Nauru, Papua New Guinea, Rwanda, San Marino, Sao Tome & Principe, Seychelles, Sierra Leone, Singapore, Sri Lanka, Surinam, Trinidad and Tobago, United Arab Emitates, and Upper Volta.

List #4: Prefixes and Suffixes

A. PREFIXES

Prefix	Meaning	Example
a-	not	amoral, atypical, amorphous
ab-	away from	abnormal, abrupt, abstain
ante-	before, in front of	anteroom, antecedent, antedate
anti-	against, opposite	antidote, antipathy, antiseptic
arch-	chief, prime	archbishop, archangel, archenemy
bene-	well	benefactor, benefit, benevolent
bi-	two	bisect, bifocal, bigamy
circum-	around, on all sides	circumscribe, circumnavigate, circumvent
con-		conversation, confound, convoy,
col-	with	collage, collateral, collapse,
cor-		correlate, correspond, correct,
co-		co-worker, co-exist, co-author
contra-	against, opposite	contradict, contraband, contravene
de-	not, away from, down from	descend, deflate, deviate
dis-	apart, away, not	distrust, disinterested, disorder
ex-, e-	out from, former	exit, excavate, ex-governor, egress
extra-	outside, beyond	extraordinary, extrasensory, extravagant
in-		inhale, inept, innocent,
im-	into, not	imbalance, immoral, impel,
il-		illiterate, illegal, illegible
ir-		irregular, irresponsible, irresolute

Prefix	Meaning	Example
inter-	between, at intervals	intersperse, intermittent, intervene
intra-	within	intracellular
mal-	ill, badly, bad, wrong	malfunction, malnutrition, malevolent
mis-	wrong, wrongly, not	misunderstanding, misuse, mistrust
non-	not	nonexistent, nonpayment, nonconformist
peri-	around, about, enclosing	perimeter, periscope, periphery
post-	behind, after	posterity, posthumous, postscript
pre-	before, earlier, in front of	preconceive, premonition, predict
pro-	forward, before	propulsion, prologue, project
re-	back, again	reappear, recapture, reclaim
retro-	backwards	retrospect, retroactive, retroflex
se-	aside, apart	seclusion, secede, seduce
semi-	half, partly	semiannual, semicircle, semiprecious
sub-	under, below	submarine, subnormal, submerge
super-	over, above, extra	superimpose, supernatural, superflous
syn-, sym-	together with	synchronize, synthesis, sympathy
trans-	across, over, through, beyond	transition, transcend, transgress
ultra-	beyond, excessively	ultraconservative, ultramodern, ultraviolet
uni-	one	uniform, unicameral, unique
vice-	one who takes the place of another	vice-president, viceroy, vice-counsul

B.   SUFFIXES

Noun Suffixes

Suffix	Meaning	Example
-ance, -ence -ancy, -ency	act of, state of	attendance, precedence, reliance, hesitancy, presidency, consistency
-ation	state, action, institution	fixation, exploration, starvation, foundation, organization
-dom	domain, condition of,	freedom, wisdom, kingdom
-er -or		painter, receiver, baker actor, governor, inspector
-ar	one who	bursar, liar, beggar
-eer		profiteer, racketeer, pamphleteer
-ist		segregationist, realist, cyclist
-ess		actress, poetess, lioness
-hood	state of	boyhood, falsehood, manhood
-ism	doctrine, point of view	mannerism, idealism, realism
-ity	state, quality	sanity, rapidity, elasticity
-ment	state, quality, act of	amazement, payment, embodiment
-ness	state of	fullness, shyness, sickness
-ocracy	system of government	democracy, autocracy, plutocracy
-ship	state, condition	friendship, dictatorship, membership

Adjective Suffixes

Suffix	Meaning	Example
-able, -ible	capable of	capable, edible, visible
-al	like, pertaining to	criminal, practical, musical
-ful	full of, having	useful, hopeful, successful

-ish	like,	foolish, childish, selfish
-ic	pertaining to	democratic, heroic, specific
-ive		active, explosive, sensitive
-less	without	speechless, childless, harmless
-like	having the qualities of	childlike, cowlike, statesmanlike
-ly	having the qualities of	beastly, manly, wordly
-ous	pertaining to, like	courageous, ambitious, grievous

Adverb Suffixes

Suffix	Meaning	Example
-ly	in a ... manner	happily, strangely, comically
-ward(s)	manner and direction of movement	backward(s), earthward, homeward
-wise	in the manner of	crabwise, clockwise, corkscrew-wise
	as far as .... is concerned	education-wise, weather-wise

Verb Suffixes

Suffix	Meaning	Example
-en	to become, make	deafen, ripen, widen
-ify	to cause, make	beautify, diversity, simplify
-ize	to cause, make	symbolize, hospitalize, publicize

List #5: Roots

A. LATIN

Root	Meaning	Example
agr	field, farm	agriculture, agronomy
aud	hear	auditorium, audience
aqua	water	aquatic, aqueduct
cid	kill	suicide, genocide
celer	speed, hasten	accelerate, celerity
clud, clus	close, shut	seclusion, include
cur, curr	run	incur, current
dict	say	diction, contradict
duct	lead	induce, abduct
fact	make, do	manufacture, factory
flect	bend	inflection, deflect
frater	brother	fraternal, fratricide
fund, fus	pour	refund, effusive
gress, grad	go, step	progress, gradual
jud	judgement	judicial, judicious
lect, leg	read, choose	collect, legend
loq, loc	speak	eloquent, locution
manu	hand	manuscript, manicure
mar	sea	maritime, submarine
mater	mother	maternal, matriarch
med	middle	intermediary, medium
min	smaller, inferior	diminish, minute
mort	death	mortician, mortal
nom	name	nomenclature, nominal
pater	father	paternal, patriotic
ped, pod	foot	pedal, tripod
pend	hang, weigh	depend, ponderous
plic	fold	complicate, duplicate
port	carry	portable, import
pos, pon	place, put	postpone, position
reg, rect	rule, manage	direct, regulate

rupt	break	rupture, disrupt
scrib, scrip	write	inscribe, conscription
tact, tang	touch	tactile, tangible
vacu	empty	vacuum, evacuate
voca	call	vocal, invocation
vora	devour	voracious, carnivorous

B. GREEK

Root	Meaning	Example
anthro	man	anthropoid, misanthrope
astro	star	astrology, astronaut
auto	self	automatic, automobile
biblio	book	bibliography, bibliophile
bio	life	biology, biography
chronos	time	chronicle, chronology
demo	people	democrat, demography
geo	earth	geology, geography
glot	tongue	polyglot, glottal
gram	something written	telegram, grammar
graph	write	autograph, biography
hetero	different	heterogeneous
homo	same	homogeneous, homosexual
hydra	water	dehydrate, hydrant
kosmo	world	cosmopolitan, cosmonaut
krat	power	democrat, autocrat
logo	study	anthropology, chronology
mega	big	megaphone, megaton
micro	small	microscope, microphone
naut	sailor	astronaut, nautical
necro	death	necromancer
neo	new	neophyte, neoclassical

Root	Meaning	Example
neuro	nerve	neurology, neurotic
nomo	knowledge, law	autonomy, astronomy
patho	suffering, disease	pathetic, pathology
philo	love	philosophy, philanthropist
phobo	fear	hydrophobia, phobia
phone	sound, voice	phonology, telephone
photo	light	photography, photosynthesis
poli	city	cosmopolitan, politician
poly	many	polyglot, monopoly
psych	of the mind	psychic, psychology
scop	examine	scope, telescope
soph	wise	sophisticated, philosophy
tele	distant	telegraph, telepathy
typo	image	typical, typewriter

List #6: Verb Tenses

		SIMPLE	PROGRESSIVE	PERFECT	PERFECT PROGRESSIVE
FUTURE	+	I will walk.	You will be walking.	She will have walked.	We will have been walking.
	?	Will I walk?	Will you be walking?	Will she have walked?	Will we have been walking?
	–	I won't walk	You won't be walking.	She won't have walked.	We won't have been walking.
PRESENT	+	I walk. He walks.	I am) You are) walking. He is)	I have) walked. He has)	I have) been walking. He has)
	?	Do I) walk? Does he)	Am I) Are you) walking? Is he)	Have I) walked? Has he)	Have I) been walking? Has he)
	–	I do) not walk. He does)	I am) not walking. You are)	I have) not walked. He has)	I have) not been He has) walking.
PAST	+	I walked.	I was) walking. You were)	I had walked.	I had been walking.
	?	Did I walk?	Was I) walking? Were you)	Had I walked?	Had I been walking?
	–	I didn't walk.	I was) not walking. You were)	I had not walked.	I hadn't been walking.

-33-

List #7:   Stative Verbs (22)*

appear	note
be	notice
believe	owe
belong	own
cost	prefer
feel	remember
forget	resemble
hate	see
have	seem
hear	smell
know	taste
like	think
look like	understand
love	want
mean	weigh
need	wish

*Number represents step in Grammatical Sequence (p. 11).

List #8: Non-Countable Nouns* (29)**

A. Abstract	B. Matter, material
advice	air
age	beer
beauty	blood
capitalism	bread
communism	butter
democracy	cake
energy	chalk
fun	cheese
happiness	coal
help	coffee
honesty	electricity
information	fog
justice	fish
kindness	gold
knowledge	grass
laughter	hair
liberty	ice
life	ink
play	iron
recreation	juice
strength	lumber
trouble	meat
truth	milk
virtue	oil
wisdom	oxygen
work	paper
youth	rain
	rice
	smoke
	snow
	soap
	soup
	sugar
	tea
	water
	wine
	wood

*This list is far from complete; it is intended only to be suggestive. We have tried to include high-frequency nouns. Add your own to our lists.

**Number represents step in Grammatical Sequence (p. 11).

C.   Generic terms

   business
   change
   equipment
   fruit
   furniture
   jewelry
   luggage
   machinery
   mail
   money
   news
   propaganda
   scenery
   slang
   stationery
   traffic
   vegetation
   weather

   _____
   _____
   _____
   _____
   _____
   _____
   _____
   _____
   _____
   _____
   _____
   _____

D.   Subject matter

   architecture
   art
   chemistry
   civics
   economics
   engineering
   English
   geology
   grammar
   history
   literature
   mathematics
   music
   philosophy
   physics
   science
   technology
   vocabulary

   _____
   _____
   _____
   _____
   _____
   _____
   _____
   _____
   _____
   _____
   _____
   _____

E.   Sports and recreation

F.   Countable and non-countable nouns*

E. Sports and recreation	F. Countable and non-countable nouns*
baseball	age
basketball	baseball (and other balls)
bridge	beer (and other drinks)
camping	business
dancing	change
drinking	company
football	dope
golf	glass
hiking	iron
hockey	paper
homework	play
hunting	room
opera	smoke
sailing	tape
singing	tea (party)
softball	work
swimming	youth
television	_____
traveling	_____
volleyball	_____
_____	_____
_____	_____
_____	_____
_____	_____
_____	_____
_____	_____
_____	_____

*This list consists of words that have dual meanings: one countable meaning and a different non-count meaning.

<u>List #9</u>:   <u>Frequency</u> <u>Adverbs</u> (49)*

always	seldom
perpetually	rarely
almost always/nearly always	hardly ever
invariably	scarcely ever
constantly	almost never/nearly never
usually	never
ordinarily	
habitually	ever
generally	
frequently	
often	
sometimes	
periodically	
occasionally	
infrequently	

---

*Number represents step in <u>Grammatical</u> <u>Sequence</u> (p. 12).

List #10:   Irregular Verbs

Simple	Past	Past Participle

IRREGULAR VERBS that do not change:

bet	bet	bet
bid	bid	bid
burst	burst	burst
cost	cost	cost
cut	cut	cut
hit	hit	hit
hurt	hurt	hurt
let	let	let
put	put	put
quit	quit	quit
rid	rid	rid
set	set	set
shut	shut	shut
spread	spread	spread
wet	wet	wet

IRREGULAR VERBS that change to D:

flee	fled	fled
have	had	had
hear	heard	heard
lay	laid	laid
make	made	made
pay	paid	paid
say	said	said
sell	sold	sold
tell	told	told

IRREGULAR VERBS that change to T:

bring	brought	brought
buy	bought	bought
catch	caught	caught
creep	crept	crept
deal	dealt	dealt
fight	fought	fought
feel	felt	felt
keep	kept	kept
kneel	knelt	knelt

Simple	Past	Past Participle

IRREGULAR VERBS that change to T (cont'd):

Simple	Past	Past Participle
leave	left	left
lose	lost	lost
mean	meant	meant
seek	sought	sought
sleep	slept	slept
sweep	swept	swept
teach	taught	taught
think	thought	thought
weep	wept	wept

IRREGULAR VERBS that change from D to T:

Simple	Past	Past Participle
bend	bent	bent
build	built	built
lend	lent	lent
send	sent	sent
spend	spent	spent

IRREGULAR VERBS that change the PAST PARTICIPLE to N:

Simple	Past	Past Participle
be	was/were	been
beat	beat	beaten
bite	bit	bitten
blow	blew	blown
break	broke	broken
choose	chose	chosen
do	did	done
draw	drew	drawn
drive	drove	driven
eat	ate	eaten
fall	fell	fallen
fly	flew	flown
forget	forgot	forgotten
forgive	forgave	forgiven
freeze	froze	frozen
get	got	gotten
give	gave	given
go	went	gone
grow	grew	grown
hide	hid	hidden
know	knew	known
lie	lay	lain

Simple	Past	Past Participle

IRREGULAR VERBS that change the PAST PARTICIPLE to N (cont'd.):

Simple	Past	Past Participle
ride	rode	ridden
rise	rose	risen
see	saw	seen
shake	shook	shaken
speak	spoke	spoken
steal	stole	stolen
swear	swore	sworn
take	took	taken
tear	tore	torn
throw	threw	thrown
wear	wore	worn
write	wrote	written

VERBS with a VOWEL CHANGE ONLY:

Simple	Past	Past Participle
become	became	become
bleed	bled	bled
come	came	come
dig	dug	dug
feed	fed	fed
fight	fought	fought
find	found	found
grind	ground	ground
hang	hung	hung
hold	held	held
lead	led	led
light	lit	lit
meet	met	met
read	read	read
run	ran	run
shine	shone	shone
shoot	shot	shot
sit	sat	sat
slide	slid	slid
stand	stood	stood
stick	stuck	stuck
strike	struck	struck
understand	understood	understood
win	won	won
wind	wound	wound

Simple	Past	Past Particle

VERBS with a VOWEL CHANGE from I to A to U:

Simple	Past	Past Particle
begin	began	begun
drink	drank	drunk
ring	rang	rung
shrink	shrank	shrunk
sing	sang	sung
sink	sank	sunk
spring	sprang	sprung
stink	stank	stunk
swim	swam	swum

List #11:   Direct and Indirect Objects (48, 62, 63)*

A.   Verbs that require direct object before indirect

Verbs that usually require TO**

admit	mention	report
announce	prove	say
describe	recommend	speak
explain	remember	suggest
introduce		

Verbs that usually require FOR

answer	fill	prescribe
cash	fix	pronounce
change	keep	repeat
close	open	sign
correct	prepare	translate
design		

B.   Verbs that can have indirect object before direct***

Verbs that usually require TO or Ø

bring	pass	sign
deny	pay	take
give	read	teach
hand	sell	tell
lend	send	throw
offer	show	write
owe		

Verbs that normally require FOR or Ø

build	do	leave
buy	draw	make
call	find	order
catch	get	save
cook	hire	type

---

*Numbers represent steps in Grammatical Sequence (pp. 12-13).

**Some verbs can be used with either TO or FOR, but note the difference in meaning.

***Direct object is usually not a pronoun.

List #12:   Idioms With GO (71)*

go to the beach	go partying
go biking	go to a party
go for a bike ride	go on a picnic
go boating	go riding
go bowling	go for a ride
go camping	go running
go canoeing	go for a run
go climbing	go sailing
go cycling	go for a sail
go dancing	go shopping
go drinking	go singing
go for a drink	go skating
go fishing	go skiing
go hiking	go surfing
go for a hike	go swimming
go hunting	go for a swim
go jogging	go visiting
go for a jog	go for a visit
go necking	go walking
	go for a walk

*Number represents step in Grammatical Sequence (p. 13).

List #13:   Modals

Meaning	Modal	Pres.	Fut.	Past	Similar Expression	Examples
Obligation — unavoidable	must	x	x	had to	need to, have to	We must pay our taxes by the 15th of April. You must be at school and at your desks before the bell rings.
necessity	must	x	x	had to	need have to	We had to drink brackish water in order to survive. The crops must have water soon or they will die.
prohibition	must not	x	x	it was pro-hibited	be for-bidden	You must not smoke in the arsenal. You must not play in the streets.
no obli-gation	not have to	x	x	didn't have to		She doesn't have to be at home before 10:00 p.m. They don't have to come to class.
avoidable obligation	should	x	x	should have	be supposed to	You should do your homework every day.
	ought to	x	x	ought to have		We should return these books to the library today.
Advis-ability	should	x	x	should have		You look terrible; you should see a doctor.
	ought to	x	x	ought to have		She ought to have knocked before entering.

'x' indicates that the modal is used in this time reference with no change in its form.
'-' indicates that the modal is not found in this time reference in any form.
Where the modal changes its form, the new form is indicated.

Meaning		Modal	Pres.	Fut.	Past	Similar Expression	Examples
Advis- ability (cont'd)	obligation w/implied consequences	had better	x	x	had better have		You had better pay me back before I leave. She'd better watch her language.
	strong advisability recomendation	must not	x	x	-	should not	You mustn't go out alone. It's dangerous. She mustn't drive so fast. She'll have an accident.
Preference		would rather	x	x	would rather have	would prefer, would sooner	I'd rather do it myself. He'd rather have read the book.
Ability	ability	can	x	x	could	be able to, know how to	I can speak Russian. He couldn't understand a word.
	former ability	could	-	-	could	used to, be able to	He could run a four-minute mile in those days. I couldn't express myself then.
Possibility	theoretical and/or factual	can	x	x	can have	it is possible, maybe, perhaps	Any citizen can become a senator. Could man have descended from apes? We could go to the movies tonight. The road may be blocked. He may buy a new car next year. He might have taken another road home.
		could	x	x	could have		
		may	x	x	may have		
		might	x	x	might have		

Meaning	Modal	Pres.	Fut.	Past	Similar Expression	Examples
Probability — expectation	should	x	x	should have	expect	He should be here any minute now.
	ought to	x	x	ought to have		They ought to have finished now.
inference	must	x	-	must have	have to, have got to	It's very muddy; it must have rained a lot. He's not here yet; he must be on his way.
	can't	x	-	can't have	it is not possible	She can't be hungry; she just ate.
	couldn't	x	-	couldn't have		He couldn't have flown a plane; he died in 1512.
Willingness	will	x	x	-	not mind	Stay there; I'll do the dishes.
Invitation — you	could	x	x	-	would like	Could you go to the dance with me?
	would	x	x	-	can will	Would you come to dinner tonight?
Request — he, she / we, I	may	x	x	-	can	May I leave the room?
	could	x	x	-	might	Could Johnny stay overnight?
you	would	x	x	-	can	Would you open the window?
	could	x	x	-	will	Could you please lower your voice?
Permission	may	x	x	was allowed to,	be allowed to, be permitted to	You may leave the room. She may marry whomever she likes.
	can	x	x	was permitted to		Johnny can't stay overnight.

The above chart has been adapted from work done by Mary Clark.

List #14: Two-Word Verbs

A. SEPARABLE

Verb	Meaning	Example
blow out	extinguish	The children wanted to blow out the matches.
bring up	raise children	Those parents brought their children up to respect the law.
call off	cancel	The umpire called the game off.
call up	telephone	Call me up tomorrow.
do over	do again	The teacher asked me to do the assignment over.
fill out	complete	Fill out these forms and come back tomorrow.
find out	discover	I found out what was bothering her.
give back	return	The teacher gave the papers back.
give up	abandon	We had to give up smoking.
hand in	submit	The students handed their exams in late.
hang up	place on hook	He always hangs the phone up when I'm speaking.
keep up	maintain	It costs a lot to keep that car up.
leave out	omit	I've published; don't leave that out on my resume.
let down	lower	Let your hair down.
look over	review, examine	Look the test over before beginning.
look up	search for	I spend hours looking up words.
make out	distinguish clearly	The handwriting made it impossible to make out the address.
make up	compose, invent	They made up a list of people willing to contribute money.
	use cosmetics	She made up her daughter's face for the party.

Verb	Meaning	Example
pass out	distribute	The captain passed out aspirin tablets.
pick out	choose	He picked out a tie to go with his shirt.
pick up	lift, collect	Someone picks the garbage up on Tuesday.
put away	put in the customary place	Put your toys away, children.
put off	postpone	Another meeting? Let's put it off.
put on	don	It's better to put your socks on before your shoes.
put out	extinguish	The fireman put the blaze out.
take back	return	This new radio doesn't work; I'm taking it back to the store.
take off	remove	They took their coats off when they entered.
take up	raise, discuss	Take that issue up with the manager.
talk over	discuss	The defendant talked his case over with lawyers.
throw away	discard	Don't throw those old magazines away.
try on	test the fit, appearance	She never tries on clothes when she shops.
try out	test	They tried the car out and decided not to buy it.
turn down	reject, lower the volume	The boss turned down my request for a raise.
turn in	deliver, submit	The hub-cap thief turned himself in to the police.
turn off	stop power, shut off	Turn off the lights when you leave.
turn on	start power, put on	I turned the lights on to see better.
use up	finish	We've used all our sugar up.

B.   NON-SEPARABLE

Verb	Meaning	Example
call on	ask to recite	That teacher enjoys calling on sleeping students.
come back	return	She never comes back from school on time.
come over	pay a casual	Come over for lunch sometime.
come to	regain con- sciousness	She fainted from fright, but she soon came to.
get along with	have a friendly relationship with	That fellow seems to get along with everyone.
get by	succeed with a minimum effort	Do enough just to get by; that's his motto.
get over	recover	It took him weeks to get over the mumps.
get through	finish	I can never get through his exams in time.
go away	leave	Please go away; I'm busy now.
go over	review	Let's go over the battle plans again.
get up	arise	He gets up early.
keep on	continue	He keeps on talking until everyone leaves.
look for	search for	They looked everywhere for the lost child.
look into	investigate	Detectives are looking into the mysterious death.
look like	resemble	She looks like her grandmother.
look out	beware	Look out! The roof's caving in.
look up to	respect	Young boys often look up to famous athletes.
pass out	faint	The heat was so intense that many people passed out.
put up with	tolerate	He can't put up with dishonesty.
run into/ across	meet accidentally	Two old friends ran into each other on the street.

Verb	Meaning	Example
run out of	exhaust a supply	They ran out of gas in the middle of the Bay Bridge.
run over	hit by a car	The driver lost control and ran over an old man.
show up	appear	His ex-wife showed up at the marriage ceremony.
take after	resemble	He takes after his father in everything he does.
take off	leave	I can't stand this concert; let's take off.
talk back to	answer rudely	My children never talk back to me.
wait on	serve	He waits on tables for a living.

List #15:   Verbs That Are Followed By An Infinitive (97)*

A.   No object

agree	happen
appear	hope
arrange	know how
care	learn
consent	manage
decide	mean
deserve	offer
desire	promise
forget	refuse
guarantee	tend

B.   With object

advise	instruct
allow	invite
authorize	oblige
cause	order
challenge	permit
command	persuade
convince	remind
encourage	request
forbid	teach
force	tell
get	train
help	urge
hire	warn

C.   With or without object

ask	prepare
beg	want
expect	would like
need	

*Number represents step in Grammatical Sequence (p. 14).

List #16: Verbs Followed By Gerunds (98)*

admit	miss
appreciate	postpone
avoid	practice
can't help	quit
consider	recall
deny	regret
enjoy	resent
finish	resist
get through	risk
give up	stop
imagine	suggest
keep	threaten
keep on	understand
mind	

*Number represents step in Grammatical Sequence (p. 14).

List #17:   Verbs Followed By Infinitives Or Gerunds (99)*

(can) afford	intend
attempt	like
(can) bear	neglect
begin	plan
choose	prefer
continue	pretend
dislike	remember
dread	start
fail	(can) stand
hate	try
hesitate	

List #18:   Perception Verbs Followed By Simple Verb**(100)*

feel	see
hear	smell
observe	watch
notice	

---

*Numbers represent step in Grammatical Sequence (p.14).

**may also be followed by gerund.

List #19:   Participles As Modifiers*(122)**

amazing	amazed
amusing	amused
boring	bored
confusing	confused
convincing	convinced
disappointing	disappointed
exciting	excited
disgusting	disgusted
fascinating	fascinated
frightening	frightened
interesting	interested
shocking	shocked
surprising	surprised
terrifying	terrified
thrilling	thrilled
tiring	tired

*This list is given because students are frequently confused by these confusing pairs, especially as they are used to describe people.

**Number represents step in Grammatical Sequence (p. 16).

List #20:   Adjective & Preposition Combinations (129)*

interested in

good at
clever at
bad at
slow at
quick at
lucky at
surprised at
amazed at

fond of
in favor of
tired of
capable of
aware of
conscious of
confident of
ashamed of
sure of
afraid of
certain of
sick of

concerned about
happy about
careful about
excited about
glad about
worried about
sorry about

upset over
disturbed over

bored with
impressed with
annoyed with
delighted with
satisfied with
pleased with
disappointed with

accustomed to
resigned to
opposed to
used to

*Number represents step in Grammatical Sequence (p. 16).

List #21:   Verbs Taking Subjunctive (130)*

advise   propose
ask   recommend
demand   request
forbid   require
insist   suggest
prefer   urge

*Number represents step in Grammatical Sequence (p. 16).

List #22: Verb-Preposition Combinations (139)*

A. VERB & PREP & OBJ.   B. VERB & OBJ & PREP & OBJ.

agree on   add .... to/with
agree with   blame .... for
approve of   compare .... with/to
argue with   congratulate .... on/for
arrive at   explain .... to
arrive in   excuse .... for
belong to   introduce .... to
believe in   keep .... for
care for   prefer .... to
complain about   remind .... of
consent to   thank .... for
comment on   subtract .... from
consist of
count on
decide on
depend on
hear about
hear from
laugh at
listen to
look at
object to
pay for
rely on
succeed in
talk to
talk about
think about
vote for
wait for
wish for
work for

---

*Number represents step in Grammatical Sequence (p. 16).

```
┌─────────────────────────────────┐
│                                 │
│             THE                 │
│                                 │
│         COMMUNICATIVE           │
│                                 │
│           ASPECT                │
│                                 │
└─────────────────────────────────┘
```

Contents

The communicative aspect does not deal with linguistic forms (the MEDIUM) such as "go, went, gone" but outlines ways in which the language is used to send and receive MESSAGES. We have further analyzed the message into three sub-aspects that are usually present when a message is being communicated. The situation is the context in which the message is exchanged (where). The topic is the subject matter of the message (what), and the function is the manner and purpose of the message (how, why).

```
┌─────────────────────────────────────┐
│                                     │
│              Situations             │
│                                     │
└─────────────────────────────────────┘
```

The situation is a frame for communication. In its simplest sense, it places the communication at some definite, identifiable place and gives it a setting.

Most of the categories in the following pages deal with specific places. Some, however, are not specific as to place but are specific to an event or chain of events that are common and recurrent in specific places in everyday life.

It will be obvious that the list of situations also necessarily becomes a reflection of a specific culture. In this case, the list represents a generalized picture of American culture.

Situation Checklist

___ 1. Stores and Shops.

___ 2. Agencies and Services.

___ 3. Community.

___ 4. Health and Safety.

___ 5. Home.

___ 6. Recreation.

___ 7. Academia.

___ 8. Classroom.

___ 9. Travel.

___ 10. Jobs/Work.

List #1: Stores and Shops

General:

downtown
neighborhood variety store
mall
shopping center

country store
mail-order service center
flea market

Specific:

roadside vegetable stand
grocery store
supermarket
delicatessen
bakery
health food store

furniture store
appliance store
hardware store
fabric store
sewing center
carpets & draperies store
paint store

restaurant
cafeteria
snack bar
coffee shop
fast-food chain
pizza parlor

drug store
pharmacy
optician

department store
discount department store
clothing store
shoe store
thrift shop

stationery store
book store
newstand
tobacconist
music store
TV-radio store
sporting goods store
arts and crafts store
toy store
gift shop
pet shop
antique shop
jewelry store
photography store
"Green Stamp" redemption
        center
florist
beauty parlor
barber shop

List #2:   Agencies and Services

bank
post office
town/city offices
loan association
insurance agency
real estate agency
military recruiting office
travel agency
law firm
police department
fire department
Internal Revenue Service
certified public accountant office
stockbroker
telephone company business office
TV cable company office
advertising agency
auto rental agency
copy center
newspaper office
funeral parlor

dry cleaners
laundry
laundromat
shoe repair service

radio-TV repair
applicance repair
auto parts store
electrician
plumber
welding shop
auto repair shop
service station
carpenter
moving company

employment agency
day-care center
senior citizen's center
welfare office
Planned Parenthood
Hotline
Women's Crisis Center
charities

List #3:   Community

Places   Events

    city sidewalk   wedding
    park bench   reception
    public library   wake
    Catholic Church   funeral
    Protestant Church   memorial service
    Jewish Synagogue   church bazaar
                                       church supper
    Grange   bingo
    VFW
    DAR   strike
    Elks   picket line
    Eagles   demonstration
    Lion's Clubs   walk-a-thon
    Masons
    IOOF   parade
    Boy/Girl Scouts   band concert
    4-H Club   county fair
    FFA   hoedown
    American Legion   rodeo
    fraternities/sororities   auction
    PTA   flea market
    ASPCA   tag, yard, lawn sale
                                       Town Meeting
                                       political rally
                                       voting
                                       rummage sales
                                       beauty contest

List #4:   Health and Safety

Hospital

admittance
emergency room
operating room
ward/floor
maternity ward
private room

blood bank
clinic
doctor's office
dentist's office
optometrist's office
pharmacy
drug store
veterinarian's office

Emergencies

fire
robbery
accident

List #5:   Home

Locations

kitchen
bedroom
bathroom
living room
laundry
cellar
attic

den
study
nursery
garage
yard
sun porch
hall

Events and Activities

visitors
delivery men
mailman
guests
cooking
house cleaning

TV watching
doing the laundry
yard work
light repair work
babysitting
home improvement

List #6: Recreation

Places

museum
concert hall
historical site
zoo
aquarium
botanical garden
circus
campground
bathing beach
sports stadium

theatre
movie theatre
nightclub
discotheque
bar
cocktail lounge
marina
swimming pool
amusement park
national park, forest

Activities

concert
ballet
opera

board game
playing cards
watching TV
listening to radio, stereo
reading
gourmet cooking
gardening

birdwatching
jogging
weight lifting
martial arts
kite flying
sewing
painting
pottery making

fishing
hunting
hiking
camping
mountain climbing
horseback riding
bicycling
roller skating

hockey
skiing
skating

motor boating
canoeing
sailing
swimming
diving
surfing

soccer
baseball
softball
basketball
football
volleyball
croquet
tennis
badminton
squash
raquetball
handball
golf
gymnastics
track and field
bowling
frisbee

horse race
dog race
car race
long-distance running

List #7: Academia

Places	Events
administration building	baccalaureate
assembly hall	convocation
auditorium	faculty tea
book store	finals
campus police	fraternity/sorority rush
class room	graduation
chapel	hell week
dining hall, cafeteria	homecoming
dormitory	open house
field house	orientation
fraternity house	party
gym	prom
housing office	registration
lab	reunion
language lab	vacation
lecture hall	
library	Staff
locker room	
mail room	advisor
offices	coach
bursar	dean
dean	department head
foreign student advisor	dorm head
housing	instructor
registrar	librarian
R.O.T.C. headquarters	professor
sorority	tutor
student union	
theater	

Academic activities

lecture	seminar
lab	choosing a schedule
class discussion	research paper
quiz, exam	standardized test
grades	TOEFL
	Graduate Record Exam
	Law Boards

List #8:   Classroom Activities

manipulating objects
moving furniture
operating equipment
using the blackboard
using a tape recorder
using a typewriter
writing, reading and dictating
spelling bee

taking attendance
operating a language lab
body movements
games
pencil and paper work
cutting and pasting
map work

List #9:   Travel

Places

airport
train station
bus station
travel agency
ticket office
baggage office
check-in counter
immigrations
customs
baggage claim
waiting room

in flight
on the bus
in a train coach
in a train club car
in a train dining car
in a train sleeping berth
in a taxi
in a car
on a ferry

Interstate Highway
toll booth
junction with traffic light

hotel
motel
restaurant
tourist center/Chamber of Commerce

gas station
auto rental agency
auto repair shop

Some Events

flat tire
traffic violation
auto accident
parking ticket
hitch-hiking
hailing a cab

hotel check-in
hotel check-out

List #10: Jobs/Work

accountant
actor, actress
apartment manager
architect
artist, illustrator
athlete
auto salesman

baggage handler
banker
bank officer
bartender
barber
beautician
building contractor
bureaucrat
bus driver

carpenter
cashier
chambermaid
chef/cook
chiropractor
civil engineer
cobbler
computer programmer
construction worker
cowboy

delivery person
dentist
detective
diplomat
doctor

editor
electrician
elevator operator
entertainer

factory worker
farmer
fireman
fisherman

heating contractor
hotel, motel clerk
housewife

insurance agent
interior decorator

janitor
jeweler
journalist
junk dealer

lab technician
landscape architect
laundry worker
lawyer
librarian
logger

machine operator
mailman
mason
masseuer
mechanic (auto)
mover
musician

news reporter
nurse

optician
optometrist

painter (house)
parking lot attendant
pest exterminator
pharmacist
photographer
piano tuner
pilot
plumber
podiatrist
police officer
politician
post office clerk
potter
priest, minister,
    rabbi, evangelist
printer
psychiatrist
psychologist
publisher

receptionist
red cap
repairman
rubbish collector

scientist
secretary
security officer
service station
    attendant
shipping clerk
soldier
steward(ess)
store clerk
surgeon
surveyor

tailor
taxidermist
taxi driver
teacher, professor
telephone lineman
telephone operator
teller
translator
travel agent
traveling salesman
tree surgeon
trucker

upholsterer

veterinarian
volunteer

waiter, waitress
writer

zoo keeper

Topics

The topics of human conversation are virtually endless, but it is possible to predict a general list of topics that virtually every language learner will encounter at some time or another. The following lists are an attempt at a comprehensive list of basic topics.

Each topic is outlined as a vocabulary list of the words, phrases and idioms that might be encountered in a general conversation about the topic. In the case of the idioms, they are included not because they might appear in the context of a conversation, but rather because they have some semantic relationship to the topic.

It will again be obvious that the vocabulary collected under each topic is influenced by the cultural context of contemporary America.

Finally, please bear in mind that these lists are far from complete. They should be seen as basic words of fairly high frequency. You will want to add your own discoveries to our lists, and once again we welcome your additions and comments.

Topic Checklist

___ 1. Food	___ 26. Transportation
___ 2. Cooking	___ 27. Hotels
___ 3. Eating	___ 28. Restaurants
___ 4. Housing/Housekeeping	___ 29. Post Office
___ 5. Clothing	___ 30. Banks & Money
___ 6. Paraphernalia	___ 31. Recreation
___ 7. Family	___ 32. Sports & Games
___ 8. Human Relationships	___ 33. Music
___ 9. Human Qualities & Stages	___ 34. Photography
___ 10. Time	___ 35. Medicine & Health
___ 11. Weather & Climate	___ 36. Dentistry
___ 12. Geography	___ 37. Barber & Beautician
___ 13. Animals	___ 38. Cosmetics & Toiletries
___ 14. Birds	___ 39. Hygiene & Contraception
___ 15. Plants & Trees	___ 40. Office
___ 16. Language	___ 41. Business
___ 17. Thinking	___ 42. Agriculture
___ 18. Numbers & Math	___ 43. Shops & Tools
___ 19. Colors	___ 44. Law
___ 20. Shapes	___ 45. Police/Crime
___ 21. Substances & Materials	___ 46. Government/Politics
___ 22. Containers	___ 47. Media
___ 23. Emotions	___ 48. Religion
___ 24. Body & Its Functions; Vulgarities	___ 49. Education
___ 25. Manipulations	___ 50. Disasters
	___ 51. War/Military
	___ 52. Energy
	___ 53. Death

List #1: Food

Vegetables	Bread & Cereal	Spice & Flavoring	Beverages
bean	bread	cinnamon	ale
beet	biscuit	chili	beer
broccoli	cold cereal	clove	brandy
cabbage	doughnut	cocoa	coffee
carrot	grain	curry	coke
celery	muffin	ginger	juice
corn	oatmeal	herb	lemonade
cucumber	pancake	honey	liquor
lettuce	rice	mustard	punch
onion	roll	nutmeg	sanka
peas	toast	oregano	soda
pepper	waffle	pepper	soft drink
potato		salt	tea
pumpkin	**Meat**	syrup	water
radish	bacon	sugar	whiskey
spinach	beef		wine
squash	chicken		
tomato	duck	**Desserts**	
turnip	egg	brownie	
	fish	cake	
Fruit	hamburger	cupcake	
apple	hot dog	ice cream	
banana	lamb	pie	
berry	meatball	cookies	
blueberry	meat loaf	pudding	
cantaloupe	pork	sundae	
cherry	turkey		
grape		**Idioms & Expressions**	
grapefruit	**Dairy**	baker's dozen	
lemon	butter	baloney	
lime	cottage cheese	beef about	
melon	cheese	bring home the bacon	
orange	ice cream	corny	
peach	cream	cream of the crop	
pear	half and half	cry over spilled milk	
pineapple	margarine	cup of tea	
plum	milk	egg on	
prune	skim milk	fishy	
raspberry	sour cream	have one's cake and eat it	
raisin	yoghurt	not know beans	
strawberry		proof of the pudding	
tangerine		put one's eggs in one basket	
watermelon		sour grapes	
		spill the beans	
		square meal	
		take the cake	
		upper crust	

List #2:   Cooking

Equipment	Processes	Ingredients, dishes, measures	Adjectives
baking pan	add	baking soda	boiled
blender	bake	batter	broiled
bowl	beat	broth	crisp
bread pan	blend	casserole	curdled
broiler	boil	chops	fresh
burner	braise	cocktail	fried
casserole dish	brown	condiments	ground
cookbook	chill	corn meal	medium
colander	chop	cornstarch	moderate
cover	coat	cup	(oven)
double boiler	combine	dash	rare
eggbeater	cook	dough	raw
food processor	cover	dressing	ripe
frying pan	deep-fry	filling	scalloped
kettle	dice	flavor	slow (oven)
ladle	drain	flour	steamed
lid	fold in	lard	tender
measuring cup	freeze	loaf	thickened
mixer	fry	leftover	well-done
mixing spoon	grate	molasses	
oven	grease	oil	
pan	grind	pinch	
pot	knead	roast	
potato masher	mash	salad	
pressure cooker	measure	salad dressing	
recipe	melt	sauce	
rolling pin	mince	seasoning	
saucepan	mix	shell	
sifter	parboil	soup	
skillet	peel	steak	
spatula	pour	stew	
stove	refrigerate	stick of butter	
strainer	roast	stuffing	
thermometer	sauté	syrup	
whip	season	tablespoon	
	scald	teaspoon	
	sift	vinegar	
	simmer	(egg) whites	
	slice	(egg) yolks	
	spread		
	sprinkle	Idioms	
	stir	a flash in the pan	
	stir-fry	take with a grain of salt	
	toast	half-baked	
	toss	hard-boiled	
	turn	go to pot	
	whip	pot calling the kettle black	
		watered down	

List #3: Eating

Dishes and Utensils
carving knife
cup
fork
glass
gravy boat
knife
napkin
plate
platter
salad bowl
saucer
serving dish
spoon
soup bowl
soup spoon
tureen

Meals
appetizer
breakfast
brunch
buffet
course
dessert
dinner
lunch
picnic
smorgasbord
snack
supper

Verbs
chew
diet
dine
drink
eat
munch
nibble
sip
swallow
taste

Adjectives
bitter
delicious
dry
famished
full
hungry
moist
rich
sour
starved
succulent
sweet
tart
thick
thin
thirsty

Misc
baker
chef
cook
gourmet

List #4:   Housing/Housekeeping

Locales, general
building
city
community
country
development
farm
ghetto
home
house
housing development
neighborhood
quarter
residence
subdivision
suburb
town
village

Types
adobe
A-frame
apartment
cape
condominium
chalet
flat
high-rise
houseboat
hut
igloo
log cabin
manor
mobile home
palace
ranch house
salt-box
skyscraper
split-level
tenement
tent
tepee
trailer
tree house
wigwam

Construction materials
brick
cement
clapboard
concrete
glass
linoleum
log
shingles
steel
stone
wood

Parts
addition
bay
breezeway
bulkhead
ceiling
chimney
door
dormer
drive
electric sockets
ell
fireplace
floor
foundation
frame
fuse box
garage
light switch
picture window
plumbing
rafters
sill
stairs
steps
walk
wall
window
wiring
yard

Rooms
attic
basement
bath
bed
cellar
closet
den
dining room
family room
hall
kitchen
laundry room
living room
pantry
play room
porch
store room
toilet
utility room

Furnishings, equipment

ashtray
basin
bathtub
bed
      double
      twin
bunk
blanket
bookshelves/case
cabinet
carpet
chair
coffee table
cot
couch
counter
crib
cupboard
curtains
desk
dishwasher
draperies
dresser
dryer
easy chair
end table
electrical outlet
fireplace
freezer
furnace
iron
ironing board
lamp
light
linen
linoleum
love seat
oven
radio
record player
refrigerator
rug
shades
shelf
sheets
shower
sink
sofa
stereo
stove

table
television
toilet
towel
vacuum cleaner
washing machine
water heater

Activities

change
    (the linen/sheets)
clean (up)
do the dishes
do the laundry
dust
fix
hang out the laundry
make the bed
paint
pick up
polish
put away
repair
scrub
straighten (up)
sweep
vacuum
wash
wax
buy
build
furnish
insure
lease
let
mortgage
move
own
renovate
re-model
rent
sub-let

Idioms and expressions

hit home
on the house
raise the roof
wet blanket
call on the carpet
handwriting on the wall
keep up with the Joneses
pull up stakes
hit the sack
spick and span
make a clean sweep of
up/down one's alley
blind alley

List #5: Clothes

General
bathrobe
belt
blouse
bra
briefs
buckle
cap
cape
cardigan
coat
dress
dungarees
garter
girdle
gloves
hat
jacket
(blue)jeans
jumpsuit
mittens
muffler
nightgown
nylons
overalls
overcoat
pajamas
panties
pants
pantsuit
pantyhose
parka
raincoat
scarf
shirt
    dress
    sport
shorts
skirt

slacks
slicker
slip
stole
suit
sweater
sweatshirt
(neck)tie
tights
trousers
t-shirt
turtleneck
underclothes
underpants
undershirt
vest
wig

Footwear
boots
    cowboy
    dress
    hiking
clogs
flats
high heels
moccasins
overshoes
rubbers
shoes
shoelaces/strings
slippers
sneakers
socks
stockings

Sewing, parts
bobbin
button
buttonhole
cloth
collar
cuff
elastic
fabric
fringe
hem
hemline
hood
material
nap
needle
neckline
notch
patch
pattern
pin
pocket
ruffle
scissors
seam
sewing machine
size
sleeve
snap
stitch
thimble
thread
tuck
yarn
zipper

Adjectives

brand new
checkered
corduroy
cotton
dry cleanable
flannel
frayed
hand-me-down
hand washable
knit
large (sized)
loose
machine washable
medium (sized)
nylon
permanent press
plaid
polka dot
polyester
rayon
second-hand
silk
small (sized)
striped
tight
torn
velvet
washable
worn out
wool
woven

Verbs

baste
cut (out)
darn
dress
fit
gather
get dressed
grow out of (into)
hem
knit
pin up
put on
rip (out)
sew (up)
stitch
tack
take in
take off
take up
tear (out)
thread
trace
wear
wear out

Idioms and Expressions

be in someone's shoes
burn a hole in one's pocket
buttonhole someone
dolled up
handle with kid gloves
hit below the belt
keep one's shirt on
look for a needle in the haystack
lose one's shirt
on a shoestring
on pins and needles
shoe on the other foot
spin a yarn
stuffed shirt
tied to someone's apron strings
wear and tear

List #6: Paraphernalia

Nouns
bag
billfold
bobby pin
bracelet
briefcase
brooch
cane
change purse
checkbook
choker
cigar
cigarette
coin
comb
contact lens
credit card
crutches
earring
glasses
glasses case
jacknife
kerchief
key chain
key ring
keys

hair pin
handbag
handkerchief
identification
ID bracelet
lighter
matches
nailfile
necklace
penknife
pin
pipe
pocketbook
pocketknife
pocket watch
purse
ring
    engagement
    school
    signet
    wedding
tobacco pouch
umbrella
wallet
wristwatch

Idioms and Expressions
make head or tail
pipe dream
put that in your pipe and smoke it
up to snuff

List #7: Family

aunt

brother

cousin

daughter

dependent

father

foster parent

granddaughter

grandfather

grandmother

grandson

great aunt

guardian

husband

mother

(mother)-in-law

niece

nephew

sister

son

spouse

uncle

wife

baby brother/sister

big brother/sister

dad

daddy

gram

gramp

grandma

grandpa

in-laws

ma

mom

mommy

pa

pop

sis

half-

step-

adopted

adoptive

maternal

paternal

orphan

widow

widower

family tree

folks

kin

kindred

relation

relative

Idioms and Expressions

better half

chip off the old block

favorite son

List #8:   Human Relationships

People
acquaintance
antagonist
associate
boyfriend
buddy
colleague
companion
company
comrade
counselor
crony
crowd
date
disciple
enemy
fiance/fianceé
follower
friend
gang
girlfriend
guest
host
leader
lover
mate
mistress
mob
pal
partner
party
playmate
relative
roommate
team
teammate

Nouns
admiration
affection
antagonism
cooperation
competition
friendship
envy
hate
hatred
intimacy
love
marriage
rivalry
sex
teamwork

Verbs
admire
befriend
cooperate
compete
dislike
distrust
envy
hate
have sex
ignore
like
love
make love
share
trust

Idioms and Expressions
have an affair
blind date
breaking up
fair sex
fall-guy
gang up on
living together
old man (lady)
ringleader
side-kick
sponge off of
steady date
sucker
Tom, Dick and Harry

List #9:   Human Qualities & Stages

Qualities*
anxious
aggressive
aloof
artistic
attractive
bashful
beautiful
brave
cheerful
conceited
cold
complacent
cooperative
courageous
courteous
cowardly
crazy
cruel
dependable
determined
diligent
disciplined
dumb
foolish
fresh
friendly
funny
gorgeous
greedy
handsome
hard-working
helpful
humorous
ill-mannered
impolite
insane
intelligent

kind
lazy
loud
lovely
lovable
plain
pleasant
polite
pretty
quiet
reserved
romantic
rude
sane
self-conscious
selfish
sensitive
sentimental
serious
sexy
shy
stand-offish
strong
stuck up
studious
stupid
trustworthy
ugly
up-tight
weak
well-mannered

Stages
adolescent
age
aged
baby
child
childhood
childish
elderly
grownup
immature
infant
infantile
kid
juvenile
mature
middle-age
of age
old
retired
senior citizen
senile
teenager
toddler
young
young adult
youth

*Also see List #23 Emotions

List #10:   Time

Measures
second
minute
half-hour
hour
day
week
fortnight
month
year
leap year
decade
century
millenium

General measures
instant
moment
period
age
epoch
era
eon
split-second
daily
every day
weekly
monthly

Seasons
spring
summer
fall
autumn
winter

Daily
dawn
sunrise
sunup
morning
a.m.
forenoon
noon
afternoon
p.m.
sunset
sundown
twilight
dusk
evening
night
midnight

Instruments
almanac
calendar
clock
watch
wristwatch

Idioms and Expressions
behind the times
call it a day
fly-by-night
get along in years
in a jiffy
in the nick of time
in time
kill time
make a night of it
on time
the time is right
when in the world

List #11:   Weather and Climate

Nouns
air
breeze
cyclone
gale
gust
hurricane
tornado
wind

blizzard
drift
freezing rain
frost
hail
ice
sleet
snow

air mass
front
high
low

bolt
downpour
drought
drizzle
fog
lightning
mist
rain
shower
smog
squall
thunder
thunderstorm

cloud
cumulus
thunderhead

humidity
pressure
temperature
velocity

barometer
hygrometer
thermometer
forecast
weather report

Verbs
blow
cloud up
drift
drizzle
hail
lift
mist
pour
rain
snow
thunder

Adjectives
breezy
chilly
cloudy
cold
dreary
dusty
dry
foggy
freezing
frigid
frosty
hazardous
hot
humid
inclement
mild
partly (sunny, etc)
polar
rainy
severe
snowy
sunny
temperate
tropical
wet

Idioms & Expressions
bolt from the blue
break the ice
castles in the air
cats and dogs
cold snap
heat wave
hot air
make hay while the sun shines
rain on my parade
shoot the breeze
silver lining
take the wind out of
    someone's sails
three sheets to the wind
up in the air
weather the storm
windfall

List #12:   Geography

Space
comet
constellation
falling star
galaxy
meteor
meteorite
moon
nebula
orbit
outer space
planet
ring
satellite
space
star
sun
universe

Solar System
Earth
Jupiter
Mars
Mercury
Neptune
Pluto
Saturn
Uranus
Venus

Earth
Antarctic Circle
Arctic Circle
area
atoll
bay
beach
bog
brook
canal
canyon
cape
cascade
channel
chasm
cliff
coastline
continent
crater
creek

current
dam
dale
delta
desert
ditch
east
Equator
estuary
fault
field
fiord
forest
geyser
glacier
globe
gulf
gully
hedge
hill
island
isthmus
lake
latitude
ledge
longitude
marsh
meadow
mountain
north
ocean
peak
peninsula
plain
plateau
pole
pond
prairie
range
reef
reservoir
rift
river
sea
south
strait
stream
surf
swamp
tide

Tropic of Cancer
Tropic of Capricorn
undertow
valley
volcano
wave
waterfall
west

Material
dirt
earth
mud
pebble
rock
sod
soil
stone
turf

Events
avalanche
earthquake
ebb
erosion
eruption
flow
landslide

Idioms and Expressions
a stone's throw
babes in the woods
bog down
dirt cheap
down-to-earth
earthy
East is East and West is West
high and dry
leave no stone unturned
make a mountain of a mole hill
once in a blue moon
out of the woods
out of this world
over hill and dale
sell down the river
spaced out
stem the tide
stick in the mud
under the sun
win by a landslide

List #13:   Animals

Wild Animals
badger
bear
beaver
bobcat
chipmunk
cougar
coyote
deer
dolphin
fox
moose
mountain lion
otter
porcupine
porpoise
possum
raccoon
sea cow
skunk
squirrel
whale
wild cat
wolf

Reptiles
frog
lizard
newt
salamander
snake
tadpole
toad
tortoise
turtle

Rodents
bat
gerbil
guinea pig
hare
hamster
mouse
prairie dog
rabbit
rat
squirrel

Shellfish, etc
clam
crab
lobster
mussel
scallop
sea urchin
shrimp
snail
starfish

Domestic animals
cat
cow
dog
donkey
goat
horse
mule
ox
pig
pony
sheep

Fish
bass
bluegill
cod
eel
goldfish
guppy
herring
minnow
perch
pike
shark
sunfish
trout

Insects, etc
ant
aphid
bee
bug
butterfly
caterpillar
centipede
cockroach
cricket
dragonfly
grasshopper
praying mantis
spider
termite
water strider
worm

Zoo animals
alligator
bear
buffalo
crocodile
elephant
giraffe
gorilla
hippopotamus
hyena
leopard
lion
monkey
rhinoceros
tiger

Body parts
abdomen
antennae
claw
fangs
feelers
fur
hair
head
hoof
horns
legs
paw
scale
shell
snout
spine
spot
stripe
tail
teeth
thorax
whiskers
wings
wool

Dwellings
aquarium
barn
burrow
cage
cave
hutch
nest
pasture
pen
tank
trap

Groupings
band (gorillas)
bed (clams)
brood (hens)
cloud (gnats)
colony (ants)
flock (sheep)
gaggle (geese)
herd (elephants)
pack (dogs)
school (fish)
swarm (bees)
team (horses)
yoke (oxen)

Comparative Expressions
big as a whale
blind as a bat
brave as a lion
busy as a bee
crazy as a loon
dumb as an ox
fast as a jackrabbit
happy as a clam
proud as a peacock
quiet as a mouse
silly as a goose
slippery as an eel
slow as a turtle
sly as a fox
strong as an ox
stubborn as a mule
wise as an owl

drinks like a fish
eats like a horse
eats like a bird
runs like a deer
swims like a fish

Idioms and Expressions
back the wrong horse
black sheep
bull session
bum steer
let the cat out of the bag
cock and bull story
copycat
crocodile tears
cry wolf
dark horse
fish out of water
get one's goat
gift horse
go to the dogs
hold one's horses
horse around
horse of another color
in the doghouse
make a beeline for
make a monkey out of
monkey around with
pig-headed
play possum
road hog
smell a rat
snake in the grass
straight from the horse's mouth
take the bull by the horns
throw the bull
white elephant
wolf in sheep's clothing

List #14:   Birds

albatross
blackbird
bluebird
bobwhite
cardinal
catbird
chickadee
chicken
condor
cowbird
crane
crow
cuckoo
duck
eagle
egret
falcon
finch
flamingo
flycatcher
goldfinch
goose
grackle
grosbeak
grouse
gull
hawk
heron
hummingbird
jay
kingbird
kingfisher
kite
lark
loon
magpie
meadowlark
mockingbird
oriole
osprey
owl
parrot
partridge
pelican

pheasant
phoebe
pigeon
quail
raven
roadrunner
robin
sandpiper
snipe
sparrow
starling
swallow
swan
tern
thrush
titmouse
turkey
vulture
warbler
woodpecker
wren

beak
claw
egg
feather
tail
talon

Idioms and Expressions
bird in the hand
birds of a feather
chicken
cook one's goose
early bird
eat crow
feather in one's cap
kill two birds with one stone
nest egg
swan song
talk turkey
ugly duckling
water off a duck's back
wild goose chase

List #15:   Plants and Trees

Types, etc
arbor
bush
field
forest
garden
grove
hedge
orchard
park
woods
wilderness

Trees
ash
beech
birch
cedar
chestnut
elm
lilac
maple
oak
pine
spruce
willow

Fruit trees
apple
cherry
grapefruit
lemon
lime
orange
peach
pear
plum

Parts
acorn
bark
branch
bud
leaf
needle
pine cone
ring
root
sap
stump
trunk
twig

Plants
Weeds, etc
burdock
cattails
crabgrass
fern
milkweed
poison ivy

Wildflowers
buttercup
clover
columbine
daisy
dandelion
goldenrod
Indian paintbrush
lady's slipper
Queen Anne's lace
sunflower
violets

Garden flowers
chrysanthemum
daffodil
geranium
iris
lily
marigold
poppy
rose
snapdragon
sunflower
tulip
zinnia

Flower parts
anther
ovary
pistil
pollen
seed
stamen
stigma
style

Idioms and Expressions
against the grain
beat around the bush
bed of roses
grapevine
hit the hay
in a nutshell
the last straw
out on a limb
rest on one's laurels
reap what you sow
sow one's wild oats
turn over a new leaf
wallflower

List #16:   Language

Nouns
drama
etymology
grammar
journalism
linguistics
literature
phonology
poetry
semantics

adjective
adverb
article
autograph
comma
comprehension
conversation
definition
dialect
dialogue
diction
idiom
interview
jargon
meaning
monologue
narration
narrative
noun
paragraph
paraphrase
period
prayer
pronoun
pronunciation
punctuation
quotation
recitation
sentence
signature
slang
speech
spiel
style
syntax
title

usage
verb
verbiage

Verbs
abridge
call
censor
chat
communicate
comprehend
converse
cry
curse
debate
decode
define
dictate
discuss
drawl
edit
encode
entitle
erase
explain
explicate
express
gossip
interpret
interview
mean
misspell
narrate
paraphrase
pray
print
pronounce
punctuate
quote
read
recite
relate
report
respond
say
scrawl
sign
speak

spell
sputter
stammer
stutter
swear
symbolize
talk
tell
transcribe
translate
transliterate
type
utter
vow
write

Idioms and Expressions
call a spade a spade
call to order
a close call
far cry
double talk
read between the lines
sign on the dotted line
swear on a stack of Bibles
neither rhyme nor reason
talk of the town
tall story

List #17:   Thinking

Nouns	Verbs	Adjectives
analysis	analyze	analytical
attitude	appreciate	appreciative
belief	apprehend	aware of
brains	believe	brainy
certainty	brood	brilliant
comprehension	comprehend	certain
conception	conceive	clever
conclusion	conclude	conclusive
contemplation	consider	cognitive
conviction	contemplate	cognizant
decision	decide	convinced
deduction	deduct	crafty
deliberation	deliberate	decisive
experience	distinguish	deliberate
fantasy	experience	dull
feeling	fantasize	experiential
idea	feel	imaginative
image	figure out	intellectual
impression	imagine	intelligent
intellect	judge	irrational
intelligence	know	knowing
intention	learn	observant
judgement	meditate	perceptive
knowledge	memorize	pensive
meditation	note	rational
mind	notice	reasonable
notion	observe	smart
observation	perceive	stupid
perception	ponder	thoughtful
realization	realize	trusting
reason	reflect	truthful
reflection	retain	understanding
speculation	ruminate	wise
stupidity	see	witty
thinking	sense	
thought	speculate	Idioms and Expressions
truth	think	know the ropes
understanding	trust	level-headed
view	understand	make head or tail
wisdom	view	pipe dream
wit		neither rhyme nor reason

List #18: Numbers and Math

Nouns
addition
algebra
analysis
arithmetic
average
axiom
calculation
calculator
calculus
cipher
circumference
computation
computer
decimal
decimal point
diameter
division
equation
figure
formula
fraction
function
geometry
infinity
integral

logarithm
long division
median
multiplication
numeral
percentage
pi
postulate
probability
problem
proof
radius
rate
relativity
root
set
solution
square root
statistics
sum
theorem
theory
topology
trigonometry
value
variable

Verbs
add
average
calculate
compute
count
divide
double
equal
figure
formulate
multiply
solve
square
subtract
triple

Idioms and Expressions
face value
fifty-fifty
lump sum
put two and two together
second-rate
seeing double
sixes and sevens

List #19:   Colors

Primary
red
orange
yellow
green
blue
indigo
violet/purple

Secondary
beige
black
bronze
brown
buff
chestnut
chocolate
coffee
copper
emerald
gold
gray
ivory
khaki
lavender
maroon
olive
olive drab
pink
rose
ruby
silver
slate
tan
turquoise
white

Adjectives
brilliant
dark
dull
flat
flourescent
glossy
hot
light
lurid
metallic
mottled
pale
pied
vivid

Misc
rainbow
camouflage
spectrum

Paints
acrylic
enamel
finger
latex
oil
pastel
tempera
water

Idioms and Expressions
black and blue
blue, the blues
dyed in the wool
greenhorn
green with envy
in black and white
in the pink
in the red
paint the town red
red carpet
red cent
red herring
red letter day
red tape
silver lining
yellow (cowardly)

List #20:   Shapes

Nouns	Adjectives
arc	angular
arch	arched
block	blunt
circle	circular
cone	concave
cube	conical
diamond	crooked
disc	elliptical
dome	elongated
globe	flat, flattened
hexagon	globular
horseshoe	hexagonal
mound	horizontal
octagon	irregular
oval	linear
peak	long
pentagon	narrow
point	octagonal
pyramid	oval
rectangle	parallel
sphere	perpendicular
spiral	pointed
square	ragged
tip	round
triangle	rectangular
	sharp
	slender
	slim
	square
	straight
	triangular
	twisted
	warped

Idioms and Expressions
round peg in a square hole
vicious circle
odds and ends
sharp as a tack
straight as an arrow
run circles around someone

List #21:   Substances and Materials

Nouns	Adjectives
acid	abrasive
air	corroded
aluminum	corrosive
ashes	crumbly
asphalt	dull
base	durable
brass	dusty
bronze	flammable
cement	gaseous
cloth	gooey
concrete	gritty
copper	hard
dirt	impermeable
dust	invisible
earth	liquid
gas, gasoline	metallic
glue	pliable
goo	resilient
grease	rough
gunk	rubbery
kerosene	rusty
moisture	sharp
oil	shiny
ointment	slick
paste	slippery
petroleum	slimy
plaster	smooth
plastic	soft
plywood	solid
powder	soluble
rock	spongy
rubber	sticky
sand	strong
smoke	thick
soil	thin
steam	tough
steel	wet
stuff	

Idioms and Expressions
blow off steam
brass tacks
fly in the ointment
go up in smoke
lay it on thick
take a powder
scratch the surface
throw cold water on
knock on wood

tar
water
wood

List #22:   Containers

bag
barrel
basket
bottle
bowl
box
bucket
can
canister
carafe
carton
case
crate
cup
dish
flask
jar
jug
mug
pack
package
pot
sack
tin
tray
tub
vase
vessel

Idioms and Expressions
in the bag
have someone over a barrel
bottleneck
boxed in
drop in the bucket
left holding the bag
lock, stock and barrel
soapbox
windbag

List #23:   Emotions

Nouns
affection
aggravation
amusement
anger
anguish
annoyance
anxiety
awe
belligerence
bitterness
bliss
boredom
bravery
cheer
courage
craziness
dejection
delight
depression
disappointment
disgust
embarassment
enthusiasm
envy
fatigue
fear
feeling
fright
gladness
glee
greed
happiness
hope
horror
indifference
jealousy
joy
joviality
laughter
love
mood
nervousness
pain
passion
pity
pleasure
prejudice
pride

rage
regret
restlessness
sadness
sorrow
tears
temper
terror
tiredness
trouble
weariness
zest

Verbs
abhor
aggravate
agitate
amuse
anger
annoy
antagonize
bewilder
blush
bore
bother
burn up
calm
cheer up
console
cry
delight
depress
detest
disappoint
disgust
embarass
envy
excite
fatigue
fear
feel
frighten
fume
gladden
hate
hope
laugh
lament
like

love
mope
mourn
pain
please
rejoice
sadden
shake up
stir
tire
tremble
trouble
weep

Adjectives
abhorrent
abject
affectionate
afraid
aggravated
amorous
amused
angry
annoyed
anxious
apprehensive
belligerent
berserk
bewildered
bitter
blissful
bored
bothered
brave
calm
cheerful
cheery
crazy
dejected
delighted
depressed
disappointed
disconsolate
disgusted
embarassed
enthusiastic
envious
excited
fatigued

fearful
flustered
forlorn
frightened
glad
gleeful
grouchy
happy
hopeful
insane
irritated
jealous
jolly
joyful
jovial
loving
melancholy
merry
moody
mournful
nervous
painful
passionate
pleased
restless
sad
saddened
shy
sorrowful
tearful
timid
tired
troubled
upset
weary

Idioms and Expressions
at wit's end
blow one's top
fit to be tied
go to pieces
happy as a clam
hot and bothered
in a dither
make a scene
method in one's madness
out of sorts
stand-offish
tear jerker
trouble the waters

List #24:   The Body and its Functions

External
head
hair
shoulders
neck
arm
armpit
forearm
elbow
wrist
fist
hand
palm
thumb
finger
    index
    middle
    ring
    little
fingernail
chest
breast
nipple
stomach
abdomen
waist
hip
buttocks
penis
testes
testicles
anus
leg
knee
thigh
calf
shin
ankle
foot
heel
instep
sole
foot
toe
big toe
little toe

Face
forehead
eyebrow
temple
eyelash
eyelid
eye
    pupil
    iris
    white
eyeball
ear
earlobe
eardrum
cheek
nose
    nostril
    bridge
mouth
jaw
tongue
tooth
lip
chin
dimple
mustache
beard

Bones
skull
backbone
    vertebrae
    spine
collarbone
shoulder blade
ribs
pelvis
hipbone
kneecap

Insides
brain
windpipe
heart
lung
liver
kidney
intestines
appendix
bladder
vein
artery
muscle
blood
nerves
throat
tonsils
larynx
vagina
rectum

Body products
urine
feces
saliva/spit
perspiration/sweat
tears

Adjectives
pregnant
tall, short
thin, fat
muscular
skinny
plump
healthy
sick
robust
weak
strong
athletic
tight, loose
supple
lithe

Verbs	Idioms and Expressions	head and shoulders above
sit	after one's own heart	in over one's head
stand	all ears	heart-to-heart
jump	apple of one's eye	by heart
leap	give one's right arm	have a heart
hop	at arm's length	a heel
skip	with open arms	keep a stiff upper lip
run	turn one's back on	knock one's block off
twist	bad blood	lowbrow
bend	beat one's brains out	make no bones about
flex	beat one's head against a stone	by word of mouth
creep	wall	shoot off one's mouth
belch	bend over backwards	narrow-minded
burp	bite off more than one can chew	neck and neck
breathe	in cold blood	up to one's neck
gasp	brainstorm	nosey
see	waste one's breath	pay lip service to
hear	save one's breath	pay through the nose
smell	take away one's breath	pick a bone with
eat	breathe freely	pull one's leg
bite	cold feet	pull the wool over
chew	cool one's heels	someone's eyes
nibble	cut off one's nose to spite	shake a leg
spit	one's face	straight from the shoulder
defecate	eat one's heart out	a cold shoulder
urinate	eat one's words	a chip on one's shoulder
swallow	rub elbows with	by the skin of one's teeth
taste	elbow grease	get under one's skin
digest	keep an eye on	slap in the face
fornicate	see eye to eye	slip of the tongue
copulate	make eyes at	sweet tooth
menstruate	keep a straight face	take a load off one's feet
smile	keep one's fingers crossed	set one's teeth on edge
grin	first-hand	under one's thumb
laugh	foot the bill	all thumbs
giggle	put one's foot down	toe the mark
titter	put one's best foot forward	be on one's toes
cry	put one's foot in one's mouth	tooth and nail
weep	on all fours	tongue in cheek
sob	funny bone	tongue tied
sniffle	get on one's nerves	tongue twister
moan	get something off one's chest	on the tip of one's tongue
groan	guts	turn the other cheek
scowl	let down one's hair	turn up one's nose
	split hairs	watch one's step
	half-hearted	make one's mouth water
	hard headed	wet one's whistle

Vulgarities*

"Proper" term	Acceptable euphemism	Vulgarity
anus		ass hole, bung hole
breasts		boobies, boobs, knockers tits
buttocks	backsides cheeks, fanny rear end	ass, buns, butt, tail
copulate, (have) intercourse	make love	fuck, screw, lay
defecate	go to the bathroom go to the john	shit, (take a) dump (take a) crap
ejaculate		come
expectorate	spit	clam
(to be) flatulent	pass gas break wind	cut the cheese fart
masturbate		jack off, jerk off
menstruation	period time of the month	on the rag
penis		cock, dick, dong, pecker prick, shaft
testicles		balls, nuts
vagina, labia clitoris		clit, cunt, pussy, snatch twat
vomit	spit up	barf, throw up, up chuck toss (snap) your cookies

*To the teacher: These vulgarities should be taught, if at all, with warnings and care.
To the student: These vulgarities must be used very carefully since many Americans find them offensive. They are very rarely used between the sexes or with older people. If you are in doubt, don't use them.

List #25:   Manipulations

aim	put in
arrange	reverse
assemble	rap
attach	rip
bend	rub
break	scrape
close	seal
cool off, down	screw
crumble	take apart
crush	take out
cut	tap
deposit	tear
depress	thread
disassemble	throw
detach	tie
empty	tilt
flatten	tip
flex	turn off
flick	turn on
flip	twist
fold	undo
hammer	unfold
hang (up)	unhook
heat	unplug
hook	unlatch
ignite	unlock
insert	unscrew
latch	untie
level	weave
load	wipe
lock	zip
loop	
manueuver	Idioms and Expressions
mix	bump into
move	have a crush on
open	get a move on
pick (up)	make or break
pluck	go through the motions
plug in	take down a peg
plug up	twist one's arm
pound	flip one's lid
press	hang it up
pull	plug into
punch	pull no punches
push	wipe the slate clean

List #26:   Transportation

Land	People	Air
automobile	bus driver	aircraft
bus	chauffeur	airliner
bicycle, bike	coachman	airplane
cable car	conducter	balloon (hot air)
camper	engineer	glider
car	guide	helicopter
carriage	mechanic	jet
cart	teamster	light plane
chariot	truck driver	spacecraft
coach		spaceship
convertible		rocket
jeep	General	
litter	alley	
locomotive	bridge	aviator
moped	burden	co-pilot
motorcycle	cargo	flight attendant
pick-up	coal	pilot
rickshaw	diesel	steward/stewardess
sedan	engine	airport
sled	gasoline	boarding pass
sleigh	highway	baggage check
sports car	interstate	concourse
stagecoach	lane	control tower
subway	oil	engine
tanker	path	gate
tank truck	rest area	hangar
taxicab	road	luggage
train	schedule	propeller
tricycle	steam	reservation
trolly	street	runway
truck	thruway	seat
van	timetable	seat assignment
wagon	trail	ticket
	tire	window
	turnpike	wings
Animals	vehicle	
burro	wheel	
camel		
cow		
dog (sled)		
donkey		
horse		
llama		
mule		
oxen		

Sea
ark
barge
boat
canoe
cruise ship
dinghy
ferry
freighter
galley
hovercraft
kayak
lifeboat
motorboat
ocean liner
raft
rowboat
sailboat
ship
steamship
submarine
tugboat
vessel
warship
yacht

canal
channel
fleet
harbor
helm
hull
keel
lake
lighthouse
mast
oars
ocean
paddlewheel
pond
port
propeller
rapids
river
rudder
sail
sea
steering wheel
stream
white water

Verbs
arrive
check in
depart
disembark
drive
embark
fly
land
paddle
ride
sail
take off
tow
travel
walk

Idioms and Expressions
back-fire
get on the bandwagon
in the same boat
off the beaten track
burn one's bridges behind
know the ropes
meet half-way
pave the way for
water under the bridge/
      over the dam
fall asleep at the wheel
take a back seat to
run around in circles
slow boat to China
shipshape
up the creek without a paddle

List #27:   Hotels

boarding house
guest house
inn
hostel
hotel
motel
resort
tourist court

bellhop
cashier
chambermaid
desk clerk
doorman
gardener
guest
housekeeper
maid
manager
operator
room clerk
security guard
tourist

baggage
bath
bed
bill
bureau
chair
elevator
key
lobby
luggage
reservation
room
    single
    double
room service
table

convention
meeting
organization
party

Verbs
call (wake-up)
check in
check out
disturb (do not)
register
reserve
stay

Idioms and Expressions
bag and baggage

List #28:   Restaurants

Types
automat
cafe
cafeteria
coffee shop
diner
drive-in
fast-food
gourmet
luncheonette
natural foods
pizzeria/pizza parlor
snack bar
soda fountain

Personnel
baker
bartender
busboy
cashier
chef
cook
dishwasher
guest
headwaiter
host
hostess
maitre d'
manager
waiter
waitress

Nouns
appetizer
ashtray
bar
bowl
booth
buffet
chair
check
cocktail
course
cup
dessert
dish
fork
glass
gourmet
gratuity
knife

main course
meal
menu
mug
napkin
order
plate
platter
reservation
round (of drinks)
refill (of coffee)
salad bar
salt
serving
spoon
table
tablecloth
tax
tip

Verbs
dine
eat out
order
pay
prepare
reserve
tip
take out

Adjectives
a-la-carte
baked
bland
boiled
broiled
cold
delicious
dry
fresh
fried
grilled
hot
mashed
medium
overdone
rare
raw
salty
scrumptious
sliced
spicy
steamed
succulent
take-out
tasteless
tasty
to go
well-done

Idioms and Expressions
wine and dine
doggy bag
take the check
foot the bill

List #29: Post Office

Personnel
carrier
clerk
mailman
postman
postmaster
sorter

Nouns and Adjectives
address
airmail
book of stamps
book rate
box
cancellation
certified mail
C.O.D.
dead letter
envelope
first class, etc.
general delivery
junk mail
letter
lobby
magazine
mail
money order
newspaper
package
parcel post
registered mail
return address
special delivery
stamp
surface
U.P.S.
zip code

Verbs
address
cancel
deliver
fill out
forward
insure
lick
post
pick up
receive
register
seal
send
stamp

List #30:   Banks and Money

Nouns
balance
bank
bank account
bank book
bill
cash
certificate of deposit
check
checking account
coin
credit card
currency
deposit
dime
dollar
half dollar
interest
invoice
loan
money
mortgage
nickel
paycheck
penny
piggybank
quarter
receipt
safe deposit box
savings account
savings bond
silver dollar
statement
traveler's check
total
vault
window
withdrawal

Personnel
drive-in teller
executive officer
loan officer
messenger
safe deposit clerk
secretary
security guard
teller

Verbs
apply for
balance
borrow
bounce a check
cancel
cash
change
charge
close out
convert
count
credit
debit
deposit
endorse
insure
loan
overdraw
pay
put in
save
stop payment
take out
withdraw

Idioms and Expressions
bank on something
bottom dollar
one's money's worth
pass the buck
pretty penny
queer as a three-dollar bill
rain check
rubber check
flat broke
in the money
cheapskate
corner the market
make a buck
make both ends meet
I.O.U.
a man of means
penny wise and pound foolish

List #31:   Recreation

Amusements & Shows
amusement park
carnival
circus
dinner theater
disco
ice show
magic acts
movies
night club
radio
television

Arts
ballet
concert
dance
drama
exhibition
martial arts
music
painting
photography
recital
sculpture
theater

Crafts
batik
carpentry
crewel
crocheting
embroidery
knitting
needlepoint
pottery
quilting
sewing
weaving

Games (also see #32)
board games
bridge
cards
charades
checkers
chess
cribbage
crossword puzzle
jig saw puzzle
Monopoly
poker
rummy
Scrabble

Hobbies
coin collecting
gun collecting
miniatures
model building
stamp collecting

Sports (see #32)

Music (see #33)

Idioms and Expressions
put one's cards on the table
put your money on the line
put up or shut up
no dice
drawing card
go fly a kit
a flop
hit the jackpot
steal the show
ace up one's sleeve
do not pass Go

List #32:   Sports and Games

Games
archery
badminton
baseball
basketball
billiards
bowling
boxing
bicycling
canoeing
climbing
diving
fencing
figure skating
fishing
golf
gymnastics
hiking
hockey
horseback riding
hunting
jogging
mountaineering
pingpong
pool
raquetball
running
skiing
   downhill
   cross-country
soccer
softball
speedskating
surfing
swimming
tennis
track
volleyball
weight lifting
wrestling

Equipment
arrow
balance beam
baseball
bat

birdie
bow
bicycle
canoe
clubs
glove
golfball
hockey stick
horse
net
paddle
parallel bars
ping pong ball
pole
puck
racket/raquet
raquetball
reins
saddle
skates
skis
soccerball
softball
surfboard
target
tee
tennis ball
tennis racket
trampoline

Areas
arena
coliseum
country club
course
court
field
green
gymnasium
lane
pool
ring
rink
stadium
track

Verbs
aim
attack
catch
climb
coach
defeat
defend
hike
hit
hurl
jog
kick
lose

participate
pitch
place
play
punt
run
save
score
serve
tackle
take part in
tie
throw
win

Idioms and Expressions
batting average
below par
behind the eight ball
break the record
come-back
double-header
get on the ball
get to first base
go to bat for
have a lot on the ball
hook, line, and sinker
keep the ball rolling
make a hit
right off the bat
pinch hit
rain check
free-for-all
hit or miss
jump the gun
last lap
for keeps
long shot
pull one's punches
know what the score is
second wind
have a score to settle
shot in the dark
win hands down

List #33: Music

Nouns
album
alto
artist
ballad
band
bar
beat
composition
concert
conductor
concerto
disc
disc jockey (DJ)
folk song
group
hit
hymn
jazz
lyrics
measure
melody
note
piece
program
recital
record
release
rhythm
singer
solo
sonata
song
soprano
symphony
tenor
tune

Verbs
compose
conduct
croon
finger
harmonize
hum
interpret
pick
play
pluck
read (music)
record
sing
strum
toot
whistle

Types
baroque
bluegrass
chamber
classical
contemporary
country
country & western
dance
folk
jazz
modern
mood
opera
operetta
popular
religious
rock and roll
rock
rhythm and blues
spirituals
soul
symphonic

Instruments
banjo
bass
bassoon
cello
clarinet
cornet
cymbals
drums
dulcimer
electric guitar
fiddle
guitar
harp
horn
oboe
organ
mandolin
piano
saxophone
strings
synthesizer
tambourine
trombone
trumpet
tuba
viola
violin

Idioms and Expressions
face the music
fiddle around with
play second fiddle
soft-pedal
song and dance
for a song
music to one's ears
the blues

List #34:   Photography

Nouns
accessory
album
aperture
battery
duplicate
camera
canister
cartridge
case
composition
darkroom
developer
enlargement
electronic flash
exposure
film
filter
fixer
flash
flashbulb
Instamatic
lab
lens
light meter
mailer
movie
mug shot
negative
photo
photograph
Polaroid
portrait
positive
projector
print
roll (of film)
screen
shutter
sitting
slide
snapshot
speed
strap
stop bath

studio
telephoto
tripod
viewer
wide-angle

Verbs
come out
compose
develop
duplicate
enlarge
expose
focus
frame
load
mount
pose
print
process
rewind
take (a picture)

Misc
black and white
color
double exposure
flat, matte
glossy
out-of-focus
over-exposed
reflex
under-exposed
washed-out

Standard print sizes:
3½ x 5
5 x 7
8 x 10

Standard film sizes:
110
120
35 mm
8 mm
Super 8 mm } movie film

List #35:   Medicine and Health

Places and Areas
ambulance
birthing room
clinic
delivery room
emergency room
hospital
insane asylum
intensive care unit
labor room
laboratory
maternity ward ·
mental hospital
nursing home
operating room
pediatric ward
private room
recovery room
sanitarium
waiting room
ward

Equipment
adhesive tape
band-aid
bandage
bed
bed pan
cane
cast
crutches
gauze
heating pad
hot water bottle
operating table
oxygen tent
Q-tip (swab)
sanitary napkins
scalpel
stethoscope
thermometer
   oral
   rectal
tongue depressor
toothpaste
tweezers
vaporizer
wheelchair
x-ray machine

People
anesthesist
candy striper
chiropractor
dermatologist
doctor (M.D.)
general practitioner (G.P.)
gynecologist
intern
lab technician
neurologist
nurse
nurse practitioner
obstetrician
opthalmologist
orthopedic surgeon
out-patient
pathologist
patient
pediatrician
physician
podiatrist
practical nurse
psychiatrist
psychoanalyst
psychologist
radiologist
registered nurse (R.N.)
specialist
surgeon
urologist

Processes
appendectomy
blood pressure
cesarean section
D&C
delivery (of a baby)
diagnosis
EKG
examination
heart beat
hysterectomy
injection
innoculation
intensive care
observation
prognosis
pulse
sample
shot
specimen
surgery
temperature
tonsillectomy
vaccination
x-ray

Verbs
ache
admit
bleed
cough
deliver
diagnose
discharge
examine
faint
give birth
gargle
hurt
irritate
nurse
operate
pain
prescribe
recover
recuperate
relapse
swell
throw up
vomit

Medicine & Misc
antacid
antiseptic
aspirin
capsules
contraceptive
decongestant
eyedrops
laxative
nasal spray
ointment
penicillin
pill
prescription
sedative
suppository
tablet
vitamins

Problems	Diseases, etc.	Idioms and Expressions
abscess	allergy	on call
accident	angina	office hours
ache	arteriosclerosis	say "ah"
allergy	arthritis	turn your head and cough
blind	asthma	black and blue
burn	bronchitis	born with a silver spoon in
chills	bursitis	one's mouth
a cold	cancer	cough up
constipation	chicken pox	chain smoker
cough	cholera	dead as a doornail
cut	diabetes	dead to the world
deaf	diarrhea	over one's dead body
diarrhea	emphysema	one foot in the grave
dislocation	heart attack	croak
dumb	hepatitis	give up the ghost
exhaustion	hernia	hard of hearing
fever	influenza (flu)	over the hill
the flu	leukemia	kick the bucket
fracture	malaria	a new lease on life
indigestion	measles	give someone a dose of his own
injury	meningitis	medicine
infection	mental retardation	take one's medicine
inflammation	mononucleosis (mono)	nuts, nutty as a fruitcake
nausea	multiple sclerosis	go off the deep end
pain	mumps	a bitter pill to swallow
rash	neurosis	in the pink
runny nose	pneumonia	safe and sound
sore	polio	have a screw loose
sprain	psychosis	a shiner
stiff	rheumatic fever	a black eye
strain	rubella (German measles)	a shot in the arm
swollen	scarlet fever	a sight for sore eyes
virus	stroke	turn one's stomach
vomit	syphillis	under the weather
wound	tuberculosis (T.B.)	on the wagon
	ulcer	"break a leg"
		an apple a day keeps the
		doctor away
		skin and bones
		to be sick and tired
		of something

List #36:   Dentistry

Places
clinic
office
waiting room

Equipment
dental floss
drill
toothbrush
toothpaste
x-ray machine

People
dentist
dental hygienist
oral surgeon
orthodontist
receptionist

Verbs
ache
cap
clean
drill
extract
fill
pain
pull out
repair
x-ray

Misc
abcess
bicuspid
braces
bridge
buck teeth
cavity
checkup
decay
dentures
eye tooth
false teeth
front tooth
filling
incisor
jaw
molar
nerve
novocaine
root canal
wisdom tooth

Idioms and Expressions

give one's eye tooth for
cut one's teeth on
(to be) like pulling teeth

List #37:   Barber and Beautician

Nouns
afro
appointment
bangs
beard
butch
clippers
conditioner
cosmetics
crew-cut
curl
dandruff
drier
dye
haircut
hairdresser
hairpiece
manicure
moustache
pageboy
permanent
razor
razor blade
rollers
scissors
shampoo
shave
sideburns
split ends
tint
toupee
wave
whiskers
wig

Verbs
bleach
brush
clip
comb
curl
cut
dry
dye
rinse
set
shampoo
shave
tint
trim
wave

Adjectives
blonde
brunette
bushy
close
curly
dyed
frizzy
gray
long
redhead
short
straight
thick
thin
wavy

List #38:   Cosmetics and Toiletries

Nouns
after-shave lotion
cologne
comb
compact
cotton balls
deodorant
dental floss
emory board
eye-liner
eye-shadow
facial cleanser
hand cream
hair brush
hair remover
hair rinse
lipstick
mascara
mouth wash
mud pack
perfume
powder
razor (blade)
rouge
shampoo
shaving cream
skin cream
soap
tissues
toothbrush
tweezers

Verbs
apply
cut
dab
manicure
moisten
put on
shave
trim

List #39:   Hygiene and Contraception

Hygiene
douche
  concentrate
  fluid
  powder
feminine syringe
fountain syringe
feminine napkins
  sanitary napkins
mini(maxi) pads
panty liners
panty shields
sanitary belt
tampons
breast shield
nursing pads
feminine itching or
  irritation medication
feminine deodorant spray
tablets for cramps
  menstrual pain
diaretic tablets
  water pills

Contraception
contraceptive methods
and information
vasectomy/tubal ligation
oral contraceptives
  "the pill"
intrauterine device
  IUD
diaphragm with spermicide
cervicle cap
condom
  bags
  balloons
  French letters
  prophylactics
  protectives
  rubbers
  safes
  scum bags
  sheaths
  shields
  skins
vaginal spermacides
contraceptive creams
  foams
  gels
  inserts
  jellies
  suppositories
  vaginal tablets
the rhythm method
withdrawal
  coitus interruptus

gynecologist
obstetrician

family planning
planned parenthood
zero population growth

List #40:   Office

Nouns
appointment
business
carbon copy
conference
copier
department
desk
dictaphone
dictation
duplicate
envelope
equipment
files
intercom
letter
letterhead
mail
meeting
paper clip
pencil sharpener
postage meter
shorthand
stapler
stationery
supplies
telephone
tape dispenser
typewriter

Verbs
copy
dictate
file
manage
staple
take dictation
type

Personnel
assistant
boss
clerk
director
executive
manager
officer
president
receptionist
secretary
supervisor
typist
vice-president

Idioms and Expressions
take a letter
secretarial/typing pool
girl Friday
to be called on the carpet
right-hand man
business is business

List #41:   Business

People
accountant
agent
bookkeeper
chairman of the board
clerk
consultant
dealer
employee
employer
executive
investor
manager
operator
owner
partner
proprietor
salesman/woman
stockholder
worker

Types
agency
chain
company
conglomerate
corporation
dealership
franchise
holding company
industry
monopoly
organization
partnership
service
trust

Nouns
account
balance
bill
bond
books
capital
capital gains
cash
cash flow
credit
debit
debt
deduction
department
depletion
depreciation
(the) economy
excise tax
expenditure
expense account
fee
fiscal year
fringe benefit
income
interest
inventory
investment
ledger
license
loss
management
(the) market
mortgage
overhead
payroll
petty cash
profit
receipt
sales
share
social security
stock
stock market
tax
Wall Street
worksheet

Verbs
balance
borrow
buy
finance
invest
lend
liquidate
loan
sell

Adjectives
fiscal
gross
incorporated
industrial
net
private
public

Idioms and Expressions
In the black
Bullish
In the red
Bearish

List #42:   Agriculture

Nouns
acreage
agronomy
baler
barn
combine
commodity
crop
crop-dusting
cultivation
cultivator
earth
farm
farmers' market
feed
fence
field
fodder
garden
harrow
harvest
horticulture
insecticide
irrigation
implements
manure
market gardening
orchard
pasture
pesticides
pitchfork
plow
product
reaper
silage
silo
staple crops
subsidy
thresher
tiller
tractor
truck farming
wagon
well
yield

Verbs
breed
cultivate
fertilize
graze
grow
harvest
hay
irrigate
plant
plow
raise
reap
sow
weed

Crops and Products
cattle
citrus
dairy
eggs
fruit
grains
hogs
livestock
poultry
sheep
vegetables

Idioms and Expressions
cut and dried
farm out
make hay while the sun shines
40 acres and a mule
the grass is always greener on
     the other side of the fence
you reap what you sow

List #43:   Shops and Tools

Names of tools
ax, axe
bit
brace
calipers
chisel
clamp
drill
hammer
hatchet
level
mallet
plane
pliers
sander
saw
screwdriver
square
straight edge
staple gun
tape measure
tin snips
torch
vise
wedge
wire cutters
wrench

Misc
apprentice
bolt
brad
carpenter
coat (of paint)
electrician
helper
nail
nut
paint
plumber
plywood
polyurethane
primer
sandpaper
screw
shellac
spike
stain
staple
steelwool
tack
tubing
varnish
welder
wire

Verbs
bolt
build
clamp
cut
glue
hammer
measure
nail
paint
plane
pound
sand
saw
screw
scribe
solder
staple
weld

Idioms and Expressions
get the axe
have an axe to grind
hit the nail on the head
many irons in the fire
jack of all trades
live wire
nuts and bolts
handyman
on the level
to measure up

List #44:   Law

People
attorney
bailiff
clerk
counsel
court reporter
defendant
district attorney
Grand Jury
judge
juror
jury
jury foreman
lawyer
minor
offender
plaintiff
probation officer
prosecutor, prosecuting attorney
public defender
state's attorney
witness

Places and things
bar
bench
civil court
courthouse
Court of Appeals
courtroom
Federal District Court
gavel
jury box
judge's chambers
law office
legal aid service
probate court
State District Court
Supreme Court
witness stand

Adjectives
alleged
hung (jury)
guilty
innocent
judicial
legal
liable
no contest; nolo contendre
(objection) over-ruled
(objection) sustained
pre-trial

Verbs
acquit
allege
appeal
argue
award
charge
charge the jury
commute
convict
defend
deliberate
dissent
enter a plea
find
hear a case
indict
instruct
jump bail
plead
prosecute
reverse a decision
sentence
serve a sentence
sue
swear
testify
throw out a case
try
uphold

Events and Processes
accusation
acquittal
alimony
allegation
appeal
bail
case
charge
claim
conviction
court order
crime
cross-examination
damages
death penalty
decision
defense
deposition
evidence
exhibit
findings
fraud
grievance
hearing
indictment
injunction
inquiry
inquest
law
libel
litigation
manslaughter
mistrial
opinion
parole
perjury
probation
prosecution

recess
retrial
right(s)
ruling
sentence
sequester
settlement
suit
summons
testimony
trial
verdict
writ

Idioms and Expressions
bail out
do time
get away with murder
here come the judge
jailbird
lay down the law
of age
open and shut case
take the law into one's own hands
take the stand
third degree
throw the book at
under age

List #45:   Police/Crime

Good Guys
chief
constable
cop
detective
deputy
F.B.I.
game warden
investigator
meter maid
patrolman
plainclothesman
policeman/woman
private eye
private investigator
sergeant
sheriff
state trooper
traffic cop
undercoverman/woman
U.S. Marshal
warden

Bad Guys
arsonist
burglar
con man
crook
felon
fence
gang
hood
juvenile delinquent (J.D.)
killer
mafia
mugger
petty thief
pickpocket
rapist
robber
second-story man
swindler
thief
thug
tough
underworld
vandal

Events
apprehension
armed robbery
arrest
arson
assault (and battery)
break-in
burglary
chase
con game
conviction
frame-up
get-away
hold-up
homicide
investigation
line-up
mugging
mug shot
murder
rape
robbery
speeding
speed-trap
stick-up
traffic violation
vandalism

Idioms and Expressions
breaking and entering
cops and robbers
deadly weapon
fuzz
gumball machine
by hook or by crook
inside job
in the name of the law
premeditated murder
Smokey the Bear

Places
beat
cell
jail
lock-up
precint
rounds
station

Things
badge
billy club
gun
handcuffs
knife
mace
manacles
night stick
paddy wagon
pistol
revolver
siren
squad car

List #46:   Politics/Goverment

People
aide
alderman
assemblyman
attorney general
candidate
columnist
commentator
congressman
councilor
delegate
governor
incumbent
mayor
pollster
president
representative
secretary of state, etc.
selectman
senator
sheriff
speaker
vice-president
voter

Places, etc.
bill
cabinet
capitol
congress
Congressional Record
conservative
Democrat
election
hearing
inauguration
Independent
investigation
legislation
liberal
majority
minority
Pentagon
polling place
primary
Republican
State House
White House

Adjectives
executive
judicial
legislative
city
county
federal
local
national
state
town

Verbs
campaign
debate
elect
enact
filibuster
govern
lobby
pass
preside
propose
re-elect
veto
vote

List #47:   Media

Nouns
ad, advertisement
AM
announcement
audience
broadcast
bulletin
cable TV
channel
classifieds
commercial
coverage
edition
editorial
FM
interview
journal
magazine
network
news
news flash
newspaper
press
program
radio
reception
scandal sheet
scoop
station
studio
tabloid
television
transmitter
TV
UHF
VHF

Personnel
anchorman/woman
announcer
camera (man/woman) or operator
columnist
commentator
correspondent
editor
journalist
listener
newscaster
printer
producer
publisher
reader
reporter
technician
typesetter
viewer
writer

Verbs
air
announce
broadcast
print
publish
televise

Misc
commercial
daily
exclusive
illustrated
live
monthly
public
recorded
special
taped
videotaped
weekly

List #48:　Religion

Nouns
cathedral
chapel
church
meeting house
synagogue

altar boy
bishop
choir
congregation
evangelist
minister
nun
organist
pastor
Pope
priest
rabbi

altar
belfry
confession
organ
pew
steeple

bible
chatechism
hymn
prayer
psalm
sermon

baptism
christening
funeral
marriage

mass
offering
ritual
Sunday school

Verbs
believe (in)
be saved
celebrate
convert
meditate
pray
preach
worship

Denominations
Baptist
Catholic
Congregational
Christianity
Episcopal
Islam
Jehovah's Witnesses
Judaism
Lutheran
Methodist
Mormon
(Church of The
　　Latter Day Saints)
Presbyterian
Protestant
Quaker (Society of Friends)
Seventh Day Adventist
Unitarian

Adjectives
Christian
holy
Jewish
Moslem
religious
sacred
spiritual

Important days
Ash Wednesday
Christmas
Easter Sunday
Good Friday
Lent
Palm Sunday
Passover
Rosh Hashana
Yom Kippur

Idioms and Expressions
act of God
Amen!
between the devil and the
　　deep blue sea
good heavens
goodness gracious
God willing
Hallelujah
heavens to Betsy
holy Moses!
matter of faith
month of Sundays
pass the hat
raise Cain
seventh heaven

List #49:   Education

Nouns
campus
classroom
playground
school
auditorium
blackboard
gymnasium
laboratory
assignment
desk
detention
grade
homework
honor roll
lecture
recess
report card
study hall
textbook

aide
co-ed
dean
instructor
principal
professor
pupil
student
superintendent
teacher

Types of schools
elementary
graduate school
high school
junior high school
kindergarten
nursery school
preparatory (prep school)
private
secondary

Verbs
cram
enroll
fail, flunk
graduate
learn
major in
pass
study
take a course
teach

Idioms and Expressions
bone up on
burn the midnight oil
play hookey
sheepskin
teacher's pet
apple polishing

List #50: Disasters

Nouns
accidents
ambulance
blizzard
drought
earthquake
emergency
explosion
famine
fire
first aid
flood
hurricane
injury
relief
rescue
shelter
storm
tidal wave
tornado
twister
victim

Verbs
blow up
burn
collapse
crash
crush
destroy
explode
flatten
flood
freeze
injure
rescue
smash
starve

Idioms and Expressions
better safe than sorry
calm before the storm

List #51:   War/Military

Nouns	People	Idioms and Expressions
aircraft carrier	admiral	bear arms
air force	bombardier	AWOL
airplane	captain	pull rank
air raid	chaplain	stick to one's guns
armor	colonel	point blank
army	corporal	on the warpath
artillery	foot soldier	yeoman service
battle	general	all's fair in love and war
battleship	G.I.	under the gun
bomber	guerilla	
bomb	gunner	
brigade	major	
bullet	marine	
cruiser	navigator	
destroyer	oficer	
division	pilot	
fighter	sailor	
fleet	sergeant	
grenade	soldier	
gun	terrorist	
headquarters		
helicopter	Events and actions	
infantry	advance	
jeep	ambush	
jet	battle	
marines	bombardment	
mine	casualty	
missile	defeat	
navy	deploy	
regiment	inflitrate	
rocket	invasion	
shell	M.I.A. (missing in action)	
staff	offensive	
strategy	order	
submarine	over-run	
tactics	retreat	
tank	shell(ing)	
torpedo	shoot	
weapon	sink	
	skirmish	
	strafe	
	torpedo	
	wound	

List #52:   Energy

Nouns
battery
coal
combustion
conservation
consumption
electricity
engine
fire
fission
fossil fuel
fuel
fusion
gasoline
generator
heat
light
motor
natural gas
nuclear power
oil
oil well
petroleum
pollution
power
reactor
smoke
source
steam
turbine
water power
windmill

Adjectives
chemical
electric(al)
geothermal
hydroelectric
mechanical
nuclear
off-shore
passive
radioactive
solar
wood-burning

Idioms and Expressions
burn the candle at both ends
hold a candle to
carry coals to Newcastle
where there's smoke there's fire

List #53:   Death

Nouns
autopsy
body
burial
casket
cemetery
coffin
coroner
cremation
(the) deceased
demise
elegy
eulogy
funeral
funeral director
funeral procession
grave
last rites
memorial service
morgue
mortician
mourner
obituary
pall bearer
plot
(the) remains
service
tomb
undertaker
urn
vault
wake
widow
widower

Verbs
bereave
bury
cremate
die
eulogize
expire
inter
mourn
pass away

Idioms and Expressions
kick the bucket
give up the ghost
deader than a doornail
R.I.P.

```
┌─────────────────────────────────────────┐
│ ┌─────────────────────────────────────┐ │
│ │                                     │ │
│ │        Communicative Functions      │ │
│ │                                     │ │
│ └─────────────────────────────────────┘ │
└─────────────────────────────────────────┘
```

Although the sub-aspect we have labeled as Communicative Functions is similar to the functions of a notional-functional syllabus, we would like to point out that what we have proposed below is not strictly a notional-functional syllabus as we understand that term. We have used the term communicative function to draw attention to the fact that the focus of this sub-aspect is on the how and why of the communicative exchange. To relate this sub-aspect to the Situations and Topics, we can say that the Situation is concerned with the where of the exchange, the Topic the what and the Function the how and why.

To organize the various communicative functions in some useful way we have presented them as a kind of syllabus/check list. We have used as a sequential basis four levels of language sophistication. These levels represent a transition from beginning language student to fully functioning bilingual person. These four levels are:

Level 1   Surviving   (Beginner)

Level 2   Adjusting; settling in   (Advanced beginner)

Level 3   Participating   (Intermediate)

Level 4   Integrating   (Advanced)

Within each level we have organized the functions into general types as described below:

A.   Basic Needs. Using the language to satisfy basic physical requirements of food, shelter and clothing.

B.   Socializing. Using the language to forge social links with native speakers. At its lowest level it satisfies basic emotional needs.

C.   Metalinguistic. Using the language to deal with the language. Also includes certain fundamental linguistic labels and functions.

D.   Professional. Using the language to make a living.

E.   Cultural. Using the language to deal with the social and cultural milieu.

Level 1: SURVIVING

(Beginner)

A. Basic Needs

____ 1. Respond physically to simple instructions such as give, take, stand, sit, open, close, pick up, put down, put on, take off, etc.

____ 2. Give simple instructions to another to perform the actions above.

____ 3. Give and understand basic warnings such as look out!

____ 4. State basic wants and needs.

____ 5. Request and comprehend simple information.

____ 6. Ask for and respond to simple street directions.

____ 7. Interrupt someone to ask for assistance.

____ 8. Get someone's attention and also use appropriate gestures.

____ 9. Buy a small item.

____ 10. Order something to eat and drink.

B. Socializing

____ 1. Greet others.

____ 2. Take leave of another person or a group of people.

____ 3. Arrange to meet someone.

____ 4. Introduce yourself.

____ 5. Identify yourself. (I'm a _____.)

____ 6. Use ritual apologies.

____ 7. Reject unwanted attention firmly and simply.

____ 8. Agree.

____ 9. Express thanks.

____ 10. State and comprehend simple biographical information.

SURVIVING (Cont'd.)

C. Metalinguistic

____ 1.   Use and identify basic numbers.

____ 2.   Ask and tell time.

____ 3.   Use simple time expressions (today, yesterday, tomorrow morning, noon, etc.)

____ 4.   Use and comprehend days of week, months, and ways of expressing dates.

____ 5.   Control a conversation with simple phrases (speak slowly, repeat, etc.)

____ 6.   Identify and label the environment (What's that? It's a ____).

____ 7.   Decipher simple signs and notices.

Level 2:   ADJUSTING;   SETTLING IN

(Advanced beginner)

A.   Basic Needs

___   1.   State plans for the future.

___   2.   Request a loan.

___   3.   Respond to a loan request.

___   4.   Complain mildly.

___   5.   Ask about the purpose of something.

___   6.   Purchase household objects and equipment.

___   7.   Make travel arrangements.

___   8.   Describe a physical health problem.

___   9.   Carry out a limited financial transaction (cashing a check, etc.)

___   10.   Fill out life forms (credit cards, work permits, school registration, etc.)

B.   Socializing

___   1.   Introduce another person.

___   2.   Make small talk.

___   3.   Share simple likes and dislikes.

___   4.   Issue an invitation.

___   5.   Decline an invitation.

___   6.   Visit.

___   7.   Entertain a visitor.

___   8.   Play simple games/sports.

___   9.   Recount past events.

___ 10. Express basic emotions.

___ 11. Apologize for a specific error.

___ 12. Request and give permission.

___ 13. Compliment another person.

___ 14. Accept a compliment.

___ 15. Explain personal plans.

___ 16. Express a personal opinion.

___ 17. Express doubt.

___ 18. Express irritation.

___ 19. Express disappointment.

C. Metalinguistic

___ 1. Clarify misunderstandings.

___ 2. Use simple interjections.

___ 3. Make a basic phone call.

___ 4. Perform arithmetic operations.

___ 5. Spell words aloud.

___ 6. Comprehend ads and announcements on radio and TV.

___ 7. Read advertisements.

___ 8. Read short notices, time tables, menus, etc.

___ 9. Take simple dictation.

___ 10. Write short informational notes.

D. Professional

___ 1. Give simple instructions.

___ 2. Explain professional objectives.

___ 3. Express a professional opinion.

___ 4. Explain how something functions.

E. Cultural

___ 1. Follow or sing-along with popular songs and/or folk songs.

___ 2. Identify folktale characters and national heroes.

         Make general cultural comparisons in these areas:

___ 3. etiquette
___ 4. mealtimes
___ 5. kinship nomenclature
___ 6. housing
___ 7. cooking
___ 8. gift-giving
___ 9. holidays and festivals

Level 3:   PARTICIPATING

(Intermediate)

A.   Basic Needs

___ 1.   Ask for favors.

___ 2.   Grant favors.

___ 3.   Sell a personal possession.

___ 4.   Make arrangements with household help.

___ 5.   Arrange for repairs and service   (household; automotive).

___ 6.   Make substantial purchases (TV, refrigerator, etc.)

___ 7.   Apply for specific status (insurance, citizenship, etc.)

___ 8.   Retrieve a borrowed item.

___ 9.   Dispute a bill.

B.   Socializing

___ 1.   Plan a social event.

___ 2.   Attend a recreational event.

___ 3.   Discuss current events.

___ 4.   Comment on sports events.

___ 5.   Avoid commitments.

___ 6.   Sympathize.

___ 7.   Share personal hopes and dreams.

___ 8.   Tell an anecdote.

___ 9.   Understand jokes.

___ 10.   Give personal advice.

___ 11.   Disagree tactfully.

___ 12.   Ask for forgiveness.

___ 13.   Make an excuse.

C. Metalinguistic

___ 1. Understand radio and TV news.

___ 2. Break social contact with appropriate mannerisms.

___ 3. Summarize.

___ 4. Ask for definitions.

___ 5. Make a complicated telephone call.

___ 6. Translate for a new-comer.

___ 7. Swear.

___ 8. Use verbal gestures (uh-uh, hm, well, huh, etc.)

___ 9. Read newspapers.

___ 10. Read professional material.

___ 11. Read magazine articles.

___ 12. Write social notes and letters.

___ 13. Write professional reports.

D. Professional

___ 1. Allow or not allow another's requests.

___ 2. Give professional advice.

___ 3. Give detailed instructions and explanations.

___ 4. Evaluate.

___ 5. Give short talks/speeches on professional matters.

E.   Cultural

___ 1.   Explain institutions of native country.

___ 2.   Compare major cultural differences.

Discuss major aspects of host culture, including:

___ 3.   courtship

___ 4.   marriage

___ 5.   sex

___ 6.   family

___ 7.   racial and ethnic groups

___ 8.   government

___ 9.   religion

___ 10.   death

___ 11.   mourning

___ 12.   funerals

___ 13.   education

___ 14.   superstitions

___ 15.   folklore

___ 16.   hospitality

___ 17.   humor

Level 4: INTEGRATING

(Advanced)

A. Basic Needs

___ 1. Act in emergencies.

B. Socializing

___ 1. Share secrets.

___ 2. Flirt.

___ 3. Speak of personal accomplishments.

___ 4. Tease.

___ 5. Break off a relationship.

___ 6. Counsel.

___ 7. Praise.

___ 8. Flatter.

___ 9. Insult.

___ 10. Plead.

___ 11. Soften the truth.

___ 12. Chastise another person.

___ 13. Threaten.

___ 14. Tell jokes.

C. Metalinguistic

___ 1. Interpret and translate.

___ 2. Paraphrase.

___ 3. Play word games (Crossword puzzles, etc.)

___ 4. Use source materials such as Oxford English Dictionary.

___ 5. Read books.

___ 6. Write letters to the editor.

D. Professional

___ 1. Debate ideas.

___ 2. Negotiate.

___ 3. Give professional direction.

___ 4. Exercise leadership.

E. Cultural

___ 1. Take and defend a stand on a current national issue.

        Discuss, study, critique the following aspects of the culture:

___ 2. arts
___ 3. law
___ 4. attitudes toward animals and nature
___ 5. community organization
___ 6. residence rules
___ 7. property rights
___ 8. status differentiation
___ 9. social mobility
___ 10. ethics

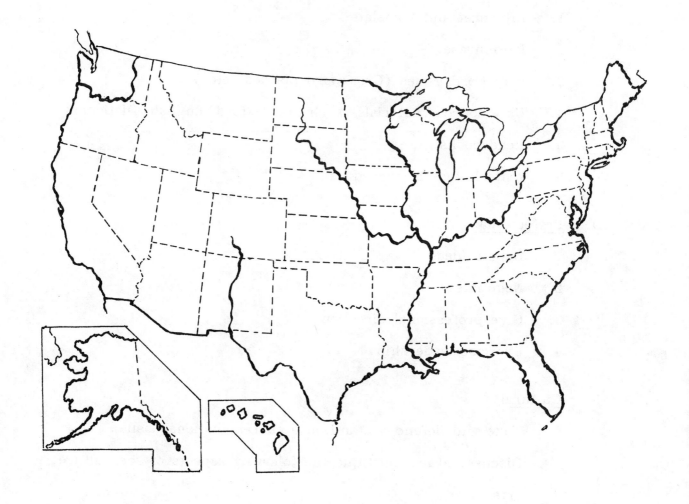

**Outline map
U.S.A.**

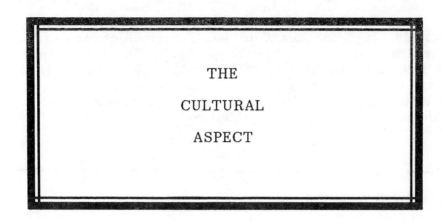

THE

CULTURAL

ASPECT

Language and culture are intertwined. In the previous section on the communicative aspect, American culture makes its presence felt, especially in the lists of communicative situations and topics. The student of another variety of English would encounter similar but decidedly different communicative situations and topics. To a lesser extent, communicative functions would also be modified by culture. Ways of expressing thanks or extending invitations can be quite different in Boston English and Bombay English.

Because we have already listed communicative situations, topics and functions in Part II, we will not repeat those lists here, but rather present cultural information that does not fit under the categories of situation, topic and function.

In other, paralinguistic ways, notably body language and gestures, culture also impinges on communication, but we will deal with that in Part V.

And then there are all the cultural practices (customs) that can only be hinted at in a book such as this. Rather than attempt to describe American cultural practices we will instead present a list of Cultural Common Denominators. This list can be used as a checklist by teacher and student to see if these areas have been adequately explored by the class.

In this part of The ESL Miscellany, we will attempt to deal with the huge body of information that is commonly known by most contemporary Americans. For example, the foreigner, unaware that the New York Yankees is a baseball team could easily be mystified by over-hearing one American ask of another, "How did the Yankees do last night?"

Obviously, it takes years to learn everything there is to know about American culture--it is even probable that some Americans do not know who Babe Ruth is. The capsule summaries of selected areas of American culture contained in this section are at best a starting point for discussion, research, explanation and study. Once again our lists should be considered only guidelines.

Checklist

____ Common Denominators

____	1.	Immigration Statistics	____ 16.	Nursery Rhymes
____	2.	Native American Population	____ 17.	Literature
____	3.	Cities of the U.S.	____ 18.	Famous Quotations
____	4.	States of the U.S.	____ 19.	Proverbs
____	5.	Industries	____ 20.	Superstitions
____	6.	U.S. Depts. & Agencies	____ 21.	Curses and Oaths
____	7.	Presidents	____ 22.	Names
____	8.	Famous Americans	____ 23.	Place Names
____	9.	Heroes	____ 24.	Religions
____	10.	Historical Sites	____ 25.	Sports Teams
____	11.	National Parks	____ 26.	Sports Personalities
____	12.	Natural Features	____ 27.	School System
____	13.	Dates and Holidays	____ 28.	Television
____	14.	Historical Dates	____ 29.	Magazines
____	15.	Folk Songs	____ 30.	National Anthem
			____ 31.	Pledge of Allegiance

Cultural Common Denominators*

Every culture has customs, traditions, practices and beliefs associated with the following cultural items. Each item in the list represents an essay, if not an entire book, but we will do no more than suggest that the list can be used as a guideline for orientation to American culture. Incidentally, the list can also serve as a checklist for a series of fascinating discussions of a cross-cultural nature.

____ numerals

____ calendar

____ personal names

____ greetings

____ gestures

____ etiquette

____ mealtimes

____ kinship nomenclature

____ age-grading

____ athletic sports

____ games

____ leisure activities

____ music

____ dancing

____ feasting

____ bodily adornment

____ folklore

____ luck superstitions

____ cooking

____ food and food taboos

____ family

____ marriage

____ kin-groups

____ housing

____ hospitality

____ visiting

____ gift-giving

____ friendship customs

____ courtship

____ joking

____ sexual restrictions

____ incest taboos

____ modesty in natural functions

____ funeral rites

____ mourning

____ medicine

____ education

____ law

____ land-use policies

____ attitude toward animals

___ community organization   ___ mobility

___ residence rules   ___ trade

___ property rights   ___ government

___ status differentiation   ___ patriotism

___ racial and ethnic groups   ___ religious practices

*Adapted from George P. Murdock, "The Common Denominators of Culture" in The Science of Man in the World Crisis, ed. Ralph Linton, N.Y.: Columbia University Press, 1945.

List #1: Immigration Statistics

Immigration by Countries: 1820 - 1978* (to nearest 100)

	1978	(1820-1978)
All countries	601,500	48,665,000
Europe	76,200	36,203,000
Austria	500 }	4,315,600
Hungary	600	
Belgium	600	202,400
Czechoslovakia	400	137,000
Denmark	400	364,200
France	2,700	750,400
Germany	7,600	6,977,700
Great Britain	16,300	4,900,000
Greece	7,000	654,900
Ireland	900	4,723,500
Italy	7,000	5,294,400
Netherlands	1,200	359,600
Norway	400	856,500
Poland	4,500	514,500
Portugal	10,500	445,400
Romania	1,600	170,900
Spain	4,300	259,600
Sweden	600	1,271,900
Switzerland	900	349,100
USSR	4,700	3,373,300
Yugoslavia	2,200	113,500
Asia	243,600	2,853,800
China	2,300	515,600
India	19,100	163,700
Japan	4,500	406,400
Turkey	1,000	385,600
Others	216,700	1,382,500

*Adapted from The Hammond Almanac, Maplewood, N.J., 1981.

America	266,500	9,050,700
Canada	23,500	4,104,900
Mexico	92,700	2,123,700
West Indies	87,700	1,686,800
Central America	20,500	312,900
South America	42,100	713,000
Africa	10,300	132,100
Australia & New Zealand	2,700	118,500
Pacific Islands	100	24,500

Percent of Total Immigrants

Years	Europe	Asia	America	Africa	Australia New Zealand	Oceania
1820-1978	74.5%	5.8%	18.5%	.3%	.2%	.6%
1961-1970	33.8%	12.9%	51.7%	.9%	.6%	.2%
1971-1978	19.3%	33.3%	45.2%	1.6%	.2%	.4%

List #2: Native American Indian Population

State	Number of Reservations	Population	Major Tribes
Alaska	13	35,817	Eskimo, Tlingit, Haida, Aleut, Athapascan
Arizona	17	173,412	Navaho, Apache, Papago, Hopi, Pima
California	76	6,908	Quechan, Hoopa, Paiute
Colorado	2	2,144	Ute
Connecticut	4	25	Pequot, Mohegan
Florida	5	1,511	Seminole, Miccosukee
Idaho	4	4,849	Shoshone, Bannock, Nez Perce
Iowa	1	561	Sac and Fox
Kansas	4	3,009	Potawatomi, Kickapoo, Iowa
Louisiana	1	268	Chitimacha
Maine	3	1,077	Passamaquoddy, Penobscot
Massachusetts	1	1	Hassanamisco-Nipmuk
Michigan	5	2,069	Chippewa, Potawatami
Minnesota	11	10,739	Chippewa, Sioux
Mississippi	1	3,194	Choctaw
Montana	7	24,137	Blackfeet, Sioux, Crow, Assiniboine, Cheyenne
Nebraska	3	2,601	Omaha, Winnebago, Santee Sioux
Nevada	23	4,784	Paiute, Shoshone, Washoe
New Mexico	24	30,125	Keresan, Zuni, Apache, Tanoan Navaho
New York	9	11,616	Seneca, Mohawk, Onondaga, Oneida
North Carolina	1	4,880	Cherokee
North Dakota	4	16,735	Chippewa, Sioux, Mandan, Arikara, Hidutsa
Oklahoma	--	80,994	Cherokee, Creek, Choctaw, Chicasaw, Cheyenne, Arapaho
Oregon	4	2,718	Warm Springs, Wasco, Paiute, Umatilla

South Dakota	8	29,119	Sioux
Texas	2	1,000	Tigua (Pueblo), Alabama, Coushatta
Utah	4	1,961	Ute, Southern Paiute, Goshute
Virginia	2	110	Algonquian
Washington	22	18,138	Yakima, Confederated, Lummi, Quinault
Wisconsin	10	7,497	Chippewa, Oneida, Winnebago
Wyoming	1	4,435	Shoshone, Arapho

List #3; Major Cities of the U.S.

(U.S. Bureau of the Census, 1980 Population)

1.	New York, N.Y.	7,071,030
2.	Chicago, Ill.	3,005,072
3.	Los Angeles, Calif.	2,966,763
4.	Philadelphia, Penn.	1,688,210
5.	Houston, Tex.	1,594,086
6.	Detroit, Mich.	1,203,339
7.	Dallas, Tex.	904,078
8.	San Diego, Calif.	875,504
9.	Baltimore, Md.	786,775
10.	San Antonio, Tex.	785,410
11.	Phoeniz, Ariz.	764,911
12.	Honolulu, Ha.	762,874
13.	Indianapolis, Ind.	700,807
14.	San Francisco, Calif.	678,974
15.	Memphis, Tenn.	646,356
16.	Washington, D.C.	637,651
17.	San Jose, Calif.	636,550
18.	Milwaukee, Wisc.	636,212
19.	Cleveland, Oh.	573,822
20.	Columbus, Oh.	564,871
21.	Boston, Mass.	562,994
22.	New Orleans, La.	557,471
23.	Jacksonville, Fla.	540,898
24.	Seattle, Wash.	493,846
25.	Denver, Col.	491,396
26.	Nasville-Davidson, Tenn.	455,651
27.	St. Louis, Mo.	453,085
28.	Kansas City, Mo.	448,159
29.	El Paso, Tex.	425,259
30.	Atlanta, Ga.	425,022

List #4: States of the U.S.

State	Date Entered Union	Capital	Electoral Vote
1. Delaware	1787	Dover	3
2. Pennsylvania	1787	Harrisburg	27
3. New Jersey	1787	Trenton	17
4. Georgia	1788	Atlanta	12
5. Connecticut	1788	Hartford	8
6. Massachusetts	1788	Boston	14
7. Maryland	1788	Annapolis	10
8. South Carolina	1788	Columbia	8
9. New Hampshire	1788	Concord	4
10. Virginia	1788	Richmond	12
11. New York	1788	Albany	41
12. North Carolina	1789	Raleigh	13
13. Rhode Island	1790	Providence	4
14. Vermont	1791	Montpelier	3
15. Kentucky	1792	Frankfort	9
16. Tennessee	1796	Nashville	10
17. Ohio	1803	Columbus	25
18. Louisiana	1812	Baton Rouge	10
19. Indiana	1816	Indianapolis	13
20. Mississippi	1817	Jackson	7
21. Illinois	1818	Springfield	26
22. Alabama	1819	Montgomery	9
23. Maine	1820	Augusta	4
24. Missouri	1821	Jefferson City	12
25. Arkansas	1836	Little Rock	6

26.	Michigan	1837	Lansing	21
27.	Florida	1845	Tallahassee	17
28.	Texas	1845	Austin	26
29.	Iowa	1846	Des Moines	8
30.	Wisconsin	1848	Madison	11
31.	California	1850	Sacramento	45
32.	Minnesota	1858	St. Paul	10
33.	Oregon	1859	Salem	6
34.	Kansas	1861	Topeka	7
35.	West Virginia	1863	Charleston	6
36.	Nevada	1864	Carson City	3
37.	Nebraska	1867	Lincoln	5
38.	Colorado	1876	Denver	7
39.	North Dakota	1889	Bismark	3
40.	South Dakota	1889	Pierre	4
41.	Montana	1889	Helena	4
42.	Washington	1889	Olympia	9
43.	Idaho	1890	Boise	4
44.	Wyoming	1890	Cheyenne	3
45.	Utah	1896	Salt Lake City	4
46.	Oklahoma	1907	Oklahoma City	8
47.	New Mexico	1912	Santa Fe	4
48.	Arizona	1912	Phoenix	6
49.	Alaska	1959	Juneau	3
50.	Hawaii	1959	Honolulu	4
	District of Columbia			3

List #5:   U.S. Industries

A.   Ranked by income:

1.   Manufacturing, durable goods (automotive, metals, machinery and electronics, wood, stone, clay and glass products)

2.   Wholesale and retail trade

3.   Services (medical, business, personal, legal, educational, hotels autos, amusement)

4.   Real estate, insurance, and banking.

5.   Government (federal, state and local)

6.   Manufacturing, consumable goods (food, chemicals, publishing, petroleum, paper, apparel, rubber and plastic, and textiles.)

7.   Contract construction

8.   Transportation

9.   Agriculture, forestry, fisheries

10.   Communication - telephone, telegraph, radio, television

11.   Electric, gas, sanitary services

12.   Mining (metal, coal, crude petroleum, minerals)

B.   State by State:

Alabama - apparel, textiles, primary metals, lumber/wood, food processing, fabricated metals, automotive tires

Alaska - oil, gas

Arizona - manufacturing, tourism, mining, agriculture (cotton, sorghum, barley, cattle)

Arkansas - manufacturing, agriculture (soybeans, rice, cotton, hay, cattle), tourism

California - agriculture (cotton, grapes, dairy products, lettuce, eggs, cattle), aerospace, manufacturing, construction, recreation

Colorado - manufacturing, government, mining, tourism, agriculture (corn, wheat, hay, sugar beets, cattle), aerospace

Connecticut - manufacturing, retail trade, government, services

Delaware - chemicals, agriculture (soybeans, corn, potatoes, mushrooms), poultry, shellfish, tourism, auto assembly, food processing, transportation equipment

Florida - services, trade, government, agriculture (citrus fruits, vegetables, sugar cane, avocados, poultry, cattle), tourism, manufacturing, aerospace, food processing, chemicals, finance, insurance, real estate, construction

Georgia - manufacturing, forestry, agriculture (cotton, peanuts, tobacco, peaches, poultry, hogs, pecans), chemicals

Hawaii - tourism, government, sugar refining, agriculture (sugar, pineapples, macadamia nuts, coffee), fishing, motion pictures, manufacturing

Idaho - agriculture (potatoes, sugar beets, alfalfa seed, wheat, barley hops, peas), manufacturing, tourism, lumber, mining, electronics

Illinois - manufacturing, wholesale and retail trade, agriculture (corn, soybeans, wheat, oats, hay, hogs, poultry, cattle), finance, insurance, real estate, publishing

Indiana - manufacturing, wholesale and retail trade, agriculture (corn, oats, wheat, soybeans, poultry, hogs), government, services

Iowa - manufacturing, agriculture (silage, feed corn, soybeans, oats, hay, cattle, hogs, poultry)

Kansas - agriculture (wheat, sorghum, corn, hay, cattle, poultry), machinery, mining, aerospace

Kentucky - tourism, agriculture (tobacco, corn, hay, wheat, fruit, cattle, chickens), manufacturing, mining, horse breeding

Louisiana - wholesale and retail trade, government, manufacturing, construction, transportation, mining, poultry

Maine - manufacturing, services, trade, government, agriculture (potatoes, apples, blueberries, sweet corn, poultry), fisheries, forestry

Maryland - government, manufacturing, fishing, services, publishing

Massachusetts - manufacturing, electronics, trade, services, education, construction, tourism, poultry

Michigan - manufacturing (automobiles, machine tools), mining, agriculture (corn, winter wheat, soybeans, fruit, poultry) food processing, tourism, fishing

Minnesota - agriculture (corn, soybeans, wheat, sugar beets, sunflowers, cattle, hogs, poultry), forest products, mining, manufacturing, tourism

Mississippi - manufacturing, food processing, seafood, government, wholesale and retail trade, agriculture (soybeans, cotton, rice, pecans, sweet potatoes, poultry)

Missouri - agriculture (soybeans, corn, wheat, cotton, cattle, hogs, poultry), manufacturing, aerospace, tourism

Montana - agriculture (wheat, barley, sugar beets, hay, flax, oats, cattle), mining, manufacturing, tourism

Nebraska - agriculture (corn, wheat, sorghum, cattle, hogs, poultry) food processing, manufacturing

Nevada - tourism (gambling), mining, manufacturing, lumber, government, agriculture (alfalfa, barley, wheat, oats, cotton), warehousing, trucking

New Hampshire - manufacturing, communications, trade, agriculture (vegetables, dairy, greenhouse products, hay, apples, poultry), mining

New Jersey - manufacturing, tourism, finance, transportation, communication, public utilities, construction

New Mexico - government, mining, tourism

New York - manufacturing, finance, communications, tourism, transportation

North Carolina - manufacturing, agriculture (tobacco, soybeans, corn, peanuts, cattle, hogs, poultry)

North Dakota - agriculture (spring wheat, durum, barley, rye, flaxseed, cattle), manufacturing

Ohio - manufacturing, tourism, government, trade, hogs, poultry

Oklahoma - manufacturing, agriculture (wheat, cotton, sorghum, peanuts, cattle, poultry), mining

Oregon - manufacturing, mining, forestry, food processing, tourism, agriculture (wheat, oats, potatoes, berries, fruits, nuts, cattle, poultry)

Pennsylvania - steel, travel, health, apparel, machinery, food processing, agriculture (corn, hay, mushrooms, fruit, winter wheat, cattle, poultry)

Rhode Island - manufacturing, services

South Carolina - tourism, textiles, apparel, chemicals, agriculture (tobacco, soybeans, corn, cotton, peaches, poultry), manufacturing

South Dakota - mining, manufacturing, agriculture (rye, flaxseed, oats, cattle, poultry)

Tennessee - manufacturing, agriculture (soybeans, tobacco, cotton, cattle, poultry), publishing, music (Nashville)

Texas - agriculture (cotton, grain, vegetables, citrus and other fruit, cattle, sheep, poultry), petroleum, manufacturing, construction

Utah - mining, manufacturing, tourism, trade, services, transportation

Vermont - manufacturing (furniture, books, scales, skiis, fishing rods), tourism, agriculture (apples, maple syrup, hay, dairy), mining, lumber, government

Virginia - government, manufacturing, agriculture (tobacco, hay, corn, peanuts, poultry), tourism, trade

Washington - aerospace, agriculture (wheat, apples, hay, potatoes, sugar beets, fruit), aluminum, lumber, trade

West Virginia - mining (coal, gas, petroleum), mineral and chemical production, agriculture (fruit, dairy, tobacco, poultry)

Wisconsin - manufacturing, trade, services, government, transportation, communications, agriculture (dairy, poultry), tourism

Wyoming - mining, agriculture (wheat, barley, oats, sugar beets, cattle, sheep), forestry, tourism

District of Columbia - government, services

List #6: U.S. Departments & Agencies

A. Departments

Department of State
Department of the Treasury
Department of Defense
Department of the Army
Department of the Navy
Department of the Air Force
Department of Justice
Department of the Interior
Department of Energy

Department of Agriculture
Department of Commerce
Department of Labor
Department of Health and
    Human Services
Department of Housing and
    Urban Development
Department of Transportation
Department of Education

B. Independent Agencies (Abridged)

ACTION (VISTA, Peace Corps, etc.)
Arms Control and Disarmament Agency

Central Intelligence Agency (CIA)
Civil Aeronautics Board (CAB)
Commission on Civil Rights
Commodity Futures Trading Commission
Consumer Product Safety Commission

Environmental Protection Agency (EPA)
Equal Employment Opportunity Commission (EEOC)
Export-Import Bank of the U.S.

Farm Credit Administration
Federal Communications Commission (FCC)
Federal Deposit Insurance Corporation (FDIC)
Federal Election Commission
Federal Home Loan Bank Board
Federal Labor Relations Authority
Federal Maritime Commission
Federal Mediation and Conciliation Service
Federal Reserve System
Federal Trade Commission (FTC)

General Accounting Office (GAO)
General Services Administration
Government Printing Office

International Communication Agency (ICA)
Interstate Commerce Commission (ICC)

Library of Congress

National Aeronautics and Space Administration (NASA)
National Capital Planning Commission
National Credit Union Administration
National Foundation on the Arts and Humanities
National Labor Relations Board
National Mediation Board
National Science Foundation
National Transportation Safety Board
Nuclear Regulatory Commission

Occupational Safety and Health Review Commission
Office of Management and Budget
Overseas Private Investment Corporation

Panama Canal Commission

Securities and Exchange Commission
Selective Service System
Small Business Administration
Smithsonian Institution

Tennessee Valley Authority (TVA)
United States International Development Cooperative Agency
U.S. International Trade Commission
U.S. Metric Board
U.S. Postal Service
Veterans Administration

<u>List #7</u>: Presidents

1. George Washington
    (1732-1799)
    Party: Federalist
    Served: 1789-1797
    Birthplace: Virginia

2. John Adams
    (1735-1826)
    Party: Federalist
    Served: (1797-1801)
    Birthplace: Massachusetts

3. Thomas Jefferson
    (1743-1826)
    Party: Democrat-Republican
    Served: 1801-1809
    Birthplace: Virginia

4. James Madison
    (1751-1836)
    Party: Democrat-Republican
    Served: 1809-1817
    Birthplace: Virginia

5. James Monroe
    (1758-1831)
    Party: Democrat-Republican
    Served: 1817-1825
    Birthplace: Massachusetts

6. John Quincy Adams
    (1767-1848)
    Party: Democrat-Republican
    Served: 1825-1829
    Birthplace: South Carolina

7.  Andrew Jackson
(1767-1845)
Party: Democrat
Served: 1829-1837
Birthplace: New York

8.  Martin VanBuren
(1782-1862)
Party: Democrat
Served: 1837-1841
Birthplace: New York

9.  William Henry Harrison
(1773-1841)
Party: Whig
Served: March-April 1841
Birthplace: Virginia

10.  John Tyler
(1790-1862)
Party: Whig
Served: 1841-1845
Birthplace: Virginia

11.  James K. Polk
(1795-1849)
Party: Democrat
Served: 1845-1849
Birthplace: North Carolina

12.  Zachary Taylor
(1784-1850)
Party: Whig
Served: 1849-1850
Birthplace: Virginia

13.  Millard Filmore
(1800-1874)
Party: Whig
Served: 1850-1853
Birthplace: New York

14.

Franklin Pierce
(1804-1869)
Party: Democrat
Served: 1853-1857
Birthplace: New Hampshire

15.

James Buchanan
(1791-1868)
Party: Democrat
Served: 1857-1861
Birthplace: Pennsylvania

16.

Abraham Lincoln
(1809-1865)
Party: Republican
Served: 1861-1865
Birthplace: Kentucky

17.

Andrew Johnson
(1808-1875)
Party: Democrat
Served: 1865-1869
Birthplace: North Carolina

18.

Ulysses S. Grant
(1822-1885)
Party: Republican
Served: 1869-1877
Birthplace: Ohio

19.

Rutherford B. Hayes
(1822-1893)
Party: Republican
Served: 1877-1881)
Birthplace: Ohio

20.

James A. Garfield
(1831-1881)
Party: Republican
Served: March-September 1881
Birthplace: Ohio

21.

Chester A. Arthur
(1830-1886)
Party: Republican
Served: 1881-1885
Birthplace: Vermont

22.

Grover Cleveland
(1837-1908)
Party: Democrat
Served: 1885-1889
Birthplace: New Jersey

23.

Benjamin Harrison
(1833-1901)
Party: Republican
Served: 1889-1893
Birthplace: Ohio

24.

Grover Cleveland
2nd Term: 1893-1897

25.

William McKinley
(1843-1901)
Party: Republican
Served: 1897-1901
Birthplace: Ohio

26.

Theodore Roosevelt
(1858-1919)
Party: Republican
Served: 1901-1909
Birthplace: New York

27.

William Howard Taft
(1857-1930)
Party: Republican
Served: 1909-1913
Birthplace: Ohio

28.

Woodrow Wilson
(1856-1924)
Party: Democrat
Served: 1913-1921
Birthplace: Virginia

19.

Warren G. Harding
(1868-1923)
Party: Republican
Served: 1921-1923
Birthplace: Ohio

30.

Calvin Coolidge
(1892-1933)
Party: Republican
Served: 1923-1919
Birthplace: Vermont

31.

Herbert C. Hoover
(1874-1964)
Party: Republican
Served: 1929-1933
Birthplace: Iowa

32.

Franklin D. Roosevelt
(1882-1945)
Party: Democrat
Served: 1933-1945
Birthplace: New York

33.

Harry S. Truman
(1884-1972)
Party: Democrat
Served: 1945-1953
Birthplace: Missouri

34.

Dwight D. Eisenhower
(1890-1969)
Party: Republican
Served: 1953-1961
Birthplace: Texas

35.

John F. Kennedy
(1917-1963)
Party: Democrat
Served: 1961-1963
Birthplace: Massachusetts

36.

Lyndon B. Johnson
(1908-1975)
Party: Democrat
Served: 1963-1969
Birthplace: Texas

37.

Richard M. Nixon
(1913-   )
Party: Republican
Served: 1969-1974
Birthplace: California

38.

Gerald R. Ford
(1913-   )
Party: Republican
Served: 1974-1977
Birthplace: Nebraska

39.

James Earl "Jimmy" Carter
(1924-   )
Party: Democrat
Served: 1977-1980
Birthplace: Georgia

40.

Ronald Reagan
(1911-   )
Party: Republican
Served: 1981-
Birthplace: Illinois

List #8: Some Famous Americans*

Alabama
Hugo Black
George Washington Carver
Nat King Cole
Helen Keller
Booker T. Washington
Hank Williams

Alaska
Vitus Bering
Joe Juneau

Arizona
Cochise
Geronimo
Barry Goldwater
Frank Lloyd Wright

Arkansas
James W. Fulbright
Douglas MacArthur

California
Luther Burbank
Wm. Randolph Hearst
John Muir

Colorado
Lowell Thomas

Connecticut
Samuel Colt
Nathan Hale
J. Pierpont Morgan
Noah Webster
Eli Whitney

Delaware
E. I. DuPont
Howard Pyle

Georgia
Martin Luther King

Hawaii
King Kamehameha

Idaho
Sacagawea

Illinois
Ernest Hemingway
Adlai Stevenson

Indiana
Hoagy Carmichael
Eugene V. Debs
Cole Porter

Iowa
Buffalo Bill Cody
Billy Sunday

Kansas
Thomas Hart Benton
John Brown
Amelia Earhart

Kentucky
Danial Boone
Kit Carson
Jefferson Davis

Louisiana
Louis Armstrong
Huey Long

Maine
Edmund Muskie
Helen Gurley Brown

Maryland
Francis Scott Key
H. L. Mencken

Massachusetts
Emily Dickinson
John Hancock
Paul Revere

Michigan
George Custer
Henry Ford

Minnesota
Walter Mondale
Harold Stassen
Bob Dylan
Judy Garland
Skitch Henderson

Mississippi
Elvis Presley
Leontyne Price
Eudora Welty

Missouri
Thomas Doolcy
John J. Pershing
Joseph Pulitzer
Sara Teasdale

Montana
Gary Cooper
Evel Knievel
Myrna Loy

Nebraska
Wm. JenningsBryan
Henry Fonda
Malcom X
Harold Lloyd

Nevada
Pat Nixon

New Hampshire
Mary Baker Eddy
Robert Frost

New Jersey
Aaron Burr
Thomas Edison
Alexander Hamilton
Paul Robeson
Molly Pitcher

New Mexico
Billy the Kid Bonney
Georgia O'Keefe

New York
Woody Allen
Art Buchwald
James Cagney
George Eastman
George Gershwin
Carl Sagan
Gloria Vanderbilt
E. B. White

North Carolina
Billy Graham
Dolly Madison
Edward R. Murrow

North Dakota
Maxwell Anderson
Lawrence Welk

Ohio
John Glenn
Bob Hope
Eddie Rickenbacker
John D. Rockefeller Sr./Jr.
Orville Wright

Oklahoma
Woody Guthrie
Oral Roberts
Will Rogers
Maria Tallchief

Oregon
Chief Joseph
Margaux Hemingway
Linus Pauling
Doc Severinsen

Pennsylvania
Marian Anderson
Andrew Carnegie
Stephen Foster
Benjamin Franklin
George C. Marshall
Betsy Ross

Puerto Rico
Pablo Casals
Roberto Clemente
José Feliciano
José Ferrer
Rita Moreno

Rhode Island
George M. Cohan
Gilbert Stuart

South Carolina
John C. Calhoun
Andrew Jackson
Eartha Kitt
William Westmoreland
Josh White

South Dakota
Calamity Jane
Crazy Horse
Sitting Bull

Tennessee
Davy Crockett
William C. Handy
Sam Houston
Dinah Shore

Texas
James Bowie
Howard Hughes
Mary Martin
Sam Rayburn

Utah
Brigham Young

Vermont
Ethan Allen
John Dewey
Stephen A. Douglas
James Fisk
Joseph Smith

Virginia
Richard Byrd
Patrick Henry
Robert E. Lee
Lewis and Clark
John Marshall
Edgar Allen Poe
Booker T. Washington

Washington
Bing Crosby
William O. Douglas

West Virginia
Pearl Buck
Thomas "Stonewall" Jackson

Washington, D.C.
Pierre Charles L'Enfant
George Washington

Wisconsin
Harry Houdini
Joseph R. McCarthy
Spencer Tracy
Orson Welles
Thornton Wilder

Wyoming
James Bridger

* Also see #7, Presidents; #9. Heroes; #26, Sports Personalities

List #9:   Heroes

A. Folk Heroes and Anti-Heroes

Horatio Alger   Wild Bill Hickock
Mohammad Ali   Howard Hughes
Johnny Appleseed   Jesse James
Sam Bass   Casey Jones
Billy the Kid   Kilroy
Bonny & Clyde   Jean Lafitte
John Brown   Charles Lindbergh
Daniel Boone   Snake Magee
Buffalo Bill   Minnehaha
Paul Bunyan   Marilyn Monroe
Al Capone   Audie Murphy
Kit Carson   Pecos Bill
Davey Crockett   Pocahontas
James Dean   Elvis Presley
John Dillinger   Paul Revere
Joe Dimaggio   Rip Van Winkle
Amelia Earhart   Will Rogers
Wyatt Earp   Babe Ruth
Evangeline   Sacagawea
Febold Feboldson   John Smith
Mike Fink   Miles Standish
Barbara Fretchie   Alfred B. Stormalong
John Henry   Tom Swift
Hiawatha   John Wayne
Wild Bill Hickock   Sergeant York
Howard Hughes

B. Comic Heroes

Alfred E. Newman   Mickey Mouse
Archie and Friends   Mutt n' Jeff
Batman and Robin   Popeye
Brenda Starr   Prince Valiant
Buck Rogers   Sad Sack
Bugs Bunny   Shazam
Captain Marvel   Snoopy
Charlie Brown   Spiderman
Dagwood & Blondie   Steve Roper
Dick Tracy   Superman
Donald Duck   Terry and the Pirates
Doonesbury   Wonder Woman
Felix the Cat   Woody Woodpecker
Flash Gordon
Fred Flintstone
Lil Abner
Mary Worth

List #10: Historical Sites

Plymouth Rock (Massachusetts)

Bunker Hill (Massachusetts)

Old North Church (Massachusetts)

Concord Bridge (Massachusetts)

Lexington (Massachusetts)

Salem (Massachusetts)

Ellis Island (New York)

Hyde Park (New York)

Liberty Bell (Pennsylvania)

Valley Forge (Pennsylvania)

Gettysburg (Pennsylvania)

Mayo Clinic (Minnesota)

Wounded Knee (South Dakota)

Mount Rushmore (South Dakota)

Boys Town (Nebraska)

Dodge City (Kansas)

The Alamo (Texas)

Fort McHenry (Maryland)

Harper's Ferry (West Virginia)

Courthouse at Appomatox (Virginia)

Mt. Vernon (Virginia)

Monticello (Virginia)

Jamestown (Virginia)

Kitty Hawk (North Carolina)

Fort Sumter (North Carolina)

The Hermitage (Tennessee)

Shiloh (Tennessee)

Andersonville (Georgia)

Cape Canaveral (Florida)

St. Augustine (Florida)

Little Big Horn (Montana)

Fort Laramie (Wyoming)

Sutter's Mill (California)

List #11:   National Parks

Acadia	Maine	1919	Rugged coastal area.
Arches	Utah	1971	Giant natural arches, windows and pinnacles shaped by erosion.
Big Bend	Texas	1944	Mountains and desert canyons of the Rio Grande
Bryce Canyon	Utah	1924	Huge amphitheater of unique erosional formations
Canyonlands	Utah	1964	Mesa country with deep canyons, spires and eroded rocks.
Capitol Reef	Utah	1971	High-walled gorges cut through sandstone cliffs.
Carlsbad Caverns	New Mexico	1930	Series of connected caverns with magnificent formations.
Crator Lake	Oregon	1902	Deep blue lake in the crater of an extinct volcano.
Everglades	Florida	1934	Subtropical wilderness with mangrove forests, open prairies and wildlife.
Glacier	Montana	1910	Superb mountain scenery with many lakes and glaciers.
Grand Canyon	Arizona	1919	Enormous gorge on Colorado River that exposes a variety of geological strata.
Grand Teton	Wyoming	1929	Series of jagged peaks and Jackson Hole--winter feeding ground of large herds of elk.
Great Smoky Mountains	N. Carolina Tennessee	1930	Diversified and luxurious plant life.
Guadalupe Mountains	Texas	1972	Lofty peaks, significant fossils and unusual flora & fauna.
Haleakala	Hawaii	1960	Rare and unusual plant and animal species within dormant volcano.
Hawaii Volcanos	Hawaii	1916	Active volcanoes; rare and luxuriant vegetation.
Hot Springs	Arkansas	1921	47 mineral springs.
Isle Royale	Michigan	1931	Largest island in Lake Superior-- home of wolves, moose and beaver.
King's Canyon	California	1940	Enormous canyons and high summits of the Sierra; giant sequoia trees.

Lassen Volcano	California	1916	Lassen Peak, recently active volcano.
Mammoth Cave	Kentucky	1926	Underground formations & river.
Mesa Verde	Colorado	1906	Prehistoric cliff dwellings.
Mount McKinley	Alaska	1917	Highest mountain in North America; large glaciers, wildlife.
Mount Rainier	Washington	1899	Large glacial system from single peak.
North Cascades	Washington	1968	Spectacular mountainous region with many glaciers, lakes.
Olympic	Washington	1909	Mountain wilderness, remnant of Pacific Northwest rain forest.
Petrified Forest	Arizona	1906	Trees that have petrified or turned to stone.
Redwood	California	1968	Coastal forest with virgin groves of giant redwood trees.
Rocky Mountain	Colorado	1975	Numerous mountain peaks.
Sequoia	California	1890	Groves of giant sequoia trees; Mount Whitney.
Shenandoah	Virginia	1926	Portion of Blue Ridge Mountains.
Theodore Roosevelt	North Dakota	1947	Roosevelt's ranch and badlands.
Virgin Islands	Virgin Islands	1956	Beaches, quiet coves.
Voyageurs	Minnestoa		Abundant lakes, forests, wildlife.
Wind Cave	S. Dakota	1903	Limestone caverns in Black Hills.
Yellowstone	Idaho, Montana, Wyoming	1872	Geyser area; lakes, waterfalls, high mountains, deep canyons.
Yosemite	California	1890	Waterfall, sequoia groves, mountains
Zion	Utah	1909	Canyon and mesa scenery.

List #12:   Natural Features

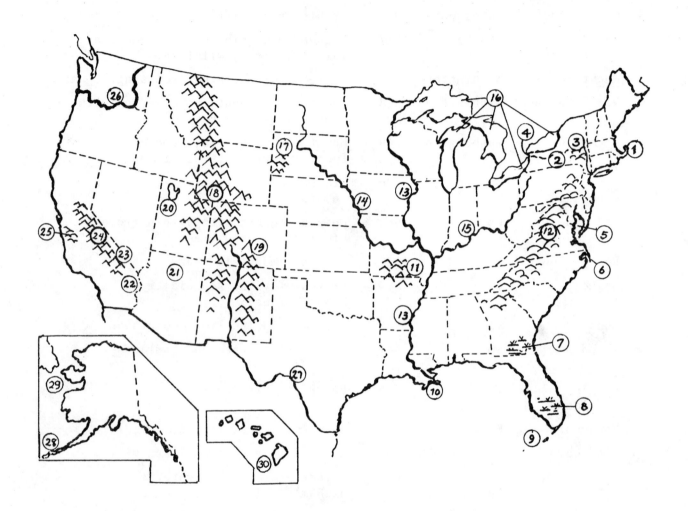

1.	Cape Cod	11.	The Ozarks	21.	Painted Desert
2.	The Erie Canal	12.	Appalachian Mts.	22.	Death Valley
3.	The Catskills	13.	Mississippi River	23.	Mt. Whitney
4.	Niagara Falls	14.	Missouri River	24.	Sierra Nevada
5.	Chesapeake Bay	15.	Ohio River	25.	Big Sur
6.	Cape Hatteras	16.	The Great Lakes	26.	Columbia River
7.	Okefenokee Swamp	17.	The Black Hills	27.	The Rio Grande
8.	The Everglades	18.	Rocky Mountains	28.	Aleutian Islands
9.	Key West	19.	Pike's Peak	29.	Bering Strait
10.	Mississippi Delta	20.	Great Salt Lake	30.	Kilauea

List #13:   Dates and Holidays

Federal Legal Public Holidays

New Years Day:	January 1
Presidents Day:	Third Monday in February
Memorial Day:	Last Monday in May
Independence Day:	July 4
Labor Day:	First Monday in September
Columbus Day:	Second Monday in October
Veterans Day:	November 17
Thanksgiving:	Fourth Thursday in November
Christmas:	December 25

Important Dates

Groundhog Day:	February 2
Lincoln's Birthday:	February 12
St. Valentine's Day:	February 14
Washington's Birthday:	February 22
St. Patrick's Day:	March 17
April Fool's Day:	April 1
Arbor Day:	Last Tuesday in April
Good Friday:	Friday before Easter Sunday
Easter Sunday:	
May Day:	May 1
Mother's Day:	Second Sunday in May
Flag Day:	June 14
Father's Day:	Third Sunday in June
Halloween:	October 31
All Saint's Day:	November 1
Sadie Hawkins Day:	First Saturday after November 11

List #14: Historical Dates

c. 1000   Leif Eriksson explores North America.

1492   Columbus explores the Carribean and publicizes the New World.

1497   John Cabot explores North America (Delaware).

1519   Cortes conquers Mexico.

1565   Spanish found St. Augustine, Florida.

1607   English found Jamestown, Virginia.

1608   French found Quebec City, Canada.

1619   First Negro laborers brought to Jamestown as indentured servants. Slavery legalized 1650.

1620   Plymouth Plantation, Massachusetts, founded by Pilgrims who came on the Mayflower.

1636   First college founded (Harvard).

1664   British seize Dutch colony of New Netherland (founded 1624) and rename it New York.

1704   First regular newspaper, Boston News Letter.

1744-   French lose Canada and Ohio Valley to British after 20 years
1763   of war. Indians fight on both sides.

1776   Colonies declare independence from Britain, July 4.

1777   First constitution (Articles of Confederation) of United States adopted.

1781   British lose the Revolutionary War (Peace treaty 1784).

1787   New Constitution of U.S.A. written and adopted.

1789   Constitution becomes official. George Washington is elected first president.

1791   Bill of Rights.

1803   U.S. under President Thomas Jefferson buys Louisiana from Napoleon.

1808   Slave importation outlawed.

1812   War with Britain.

1814   New Capitol and White House in Washington are burned by British. Peace Treaty of Ghent.

1815   British are defeated by U.S. in Battle of New Orleans after Peace Treaty. U.S. fights and defeats Barbary pirates in Mediterranean.

1823   Monroe Doctrine opposes European intervention in the Americas.

1828   "Jacksonian Revolution." The new Democratic Party under Andrew Jackson wins the presidency and takes power in Washington (the first major political change) without violence proving the stability of the U.S. government.

1846   Mexican War. U.S. takes Texas, California, Arizona, New Mexico, Nevada, Utah, Colorado, and pays Mexico $15 million.

1848   Gold discovered in California. Development of the West is accelerated.

1860   Abraham Lincoln elected.

1861   Seven southern states withdraw from U.S.A., set up Confederate States of America, and start Civil War.

1863   Lincoln legally frees the slaves in the South.

1865   Civil War ends with Northern victory. President Lincoln assassinated. 13th Amendment abolishes slavery.

1867   U.S. buys Alaska from Russia.

1869   Transcontinental railroad finished. Knights of Labor founded.

1871   Chicago fire.

1876   Custer's last stand: 265 soldiers killed by Sioux Indians.

1883   Federal Civil Service reformed by Pendleton Act.

1886   Haymarket riot and other labor unrest. American Federation of Labor (AFL) formed.

1890   "Battle" of Wounded Knee: 200 Indian men, women and children and 29 U.S. soliders killed in the last major conflict of the Indian wars.

1898   U.S. begins to take an aggressive interest in international affairs. Spanish American War to aid independence of Cuba. Spain cedes Philippines, Puerto Rico and Guam and grants freedom to Cuba. U.S. annexes Republic of Hawaii.

1899   U.S. attempts to save Chinese independence and make China an international market by declaring the Open Door Policy.

1903   U.S. fosters Panama's independence from Colombia to get treaty to build Panama Canal. Wright brothers fly first airplane at Kitty Hawk.

1906   San Francisco earthquake. Pure Food and Drug and Meat Inspection Acts.

1911   Supreme Court breaks up Standard Oil Co.

1914   The Great War in Europe. U.S. neutral. Clayton Antitrust Act spurs anti-monopoly suits by federal government.

1915	U.S. frees Haiti to make it a U.S. "protectorate." U.S. active supporting various factions in Mexican Revolution 1913-1916. U.S. hegemony expands in Carribbean.
1917	U.S. declares war on Germany. Prohibition amendment submitted; in force 1919-1933.
1918	World War I ends, November 11. Influenza epidemic in U.S. and worldwide kills 20 million.
1919	First transAtlantic flight. Russian Revolution.
1920	U.S. refuses to join League of Nations.
1924	Indians are made U.S. citizens.
1925	"Scopes Monkey Trial" dramatizes the changing understanding of evolution, science versus religion, and education in the U.S.
1926	Goddard fires first liquid fuel rocket.
1927	U.S. Marines sent into China to protect U.S. interests during civil war. Lindbergh flies Atlantic solo.
1929	"St. Valentine's Day massacre" dramatizes the power and violence of gangsters. Stock Market crash begins the Great Depression.
1932	Roosevelt initiates new "federalist" approach to solving the crisis in the U.S. economy.
1935	Committee for Industrial Organization (CIO) formed promoting stronger unions in auto, steel and other heavy industry.
1939	World War II starts in Europe. U.S. neutral but rearming and supporting Britain more and more actively (1939-1941).
1941	Japan attacks Pearl Harbor, December 7. U.S. declares war on Axis Powers (Japan, Germany, Italy).
1945	Germany surrenders, May 7. 1st atomic bomb dropped on Hiroshima, Aug. 6. 2nd atomic bomb destroys Nagasaki on Aug. 9. Japan surrenders, Aug. 15. United Nations founded.
1947	Truman Doctrine combats Communism. The Marshall Plan aids reconstruction of Europe.
1948	U.S.S.R. blockades West Berlin. British and U.S. break the blockade with an airlift. Organization of American States founded.
1949	NATO founded for mutual protection of West Europe, Canada and U.S. People's Republic of China established under Mao Tse-tung; U.S. refuses recognition and maintains relations with the Nationalist government in "exile" on Taiwan (Formosa).

1950	Korean War begins; U.N. (including U.S.) sides with South Korea against North Korea. U.S. agrees to give economic and military support to South Vietnam as well.
1953	Peace in Korea; U.S. supports anti-Communists with massive aid in Indochina War.
1954	Anti-Communist investigations by Sen. Joseph McCarthy end in his condemnation by Senate.
1955	AFL-CIO formed.
1956	Supreme Court requires schools to desegregate.
1959	Alaska and Hawaii become states.
1962	U.S. military advisors in Vietnam permitted to "fire if fired upon."
1963	President John F. Kennedy is assassinated.
1964	Major civil rights legislation proposed.
1965	President Johnson orders continuous bombing in South Vietnam and sends 184,300 troops. Riots in Watts, Los Angeles.
1966	U.S. fights in North Vietnam and Cambodia.
1967	Riots in Newark, N.J., and Detroit, Mich. 475,000 troops in Vietnam.
1968	Vietnam War peace talks begin in Paris. Martin Luther King, Jr. and Robert Kennedy assassinated.
1969	President Nixon expands the Peace Talks and begins "phased withdrawal" of U.S. Troops from Vietnam. Neil Armstrong walks on the moon.
1970	U.S. and South Vietnamese fight in Cambodia.
1972	President Nixon reopens relations with China.
1973	Vietnamese peace pacts signed.
1974	President Nixon resigns when threatened with impeachment for covering up evidence on the 1972 break-in at the Democratic National Committee offices in the Watergate in Washington.
1975	South Vietnam without U.S. military support falls to North Vietnam.
1978	U.S. agrees to hand the Panama Canal over to Panama.

List #15: Folk Songs*

Places
Dixie
The Eyes of Texas
Home on the Range
The Sidewalks of New York
The Banks of the Ohio
Shenandoah
Bury Me Not on the Lone Prairie
Red River Valley
The Streets of Laredo
Kansas City Blues
Meet Me in St. Louis, Louis
My Old Kentucky Home
Down in the Valley

Traveling & Blues
Freight Train
This Train
Midnight Special
Wanderin'
Rock Island Line
Sloop John B.
The Wabash Cannonball
Worried Man Blues

Work
I Ride an Old Paint
I've Been Working on the Railroad
Git Along Little Dogies
The Erie Canal
Drill, Ye Tarriers Drill
Blow the Man Down
When I First Came to This Land
Blow Ye Winds of Morning

For Babies and Children
Riddle Song
Hush Little Baby
Skip to My Lou
Rock-a-bye Baby
Row, Row, Row Your Boat

People
The Gambler
Sam Hall
Barbara Allen
Frankie and Johnny
Darling Corey
Sweet Betsy From Pike
Stagolee
Lily of the West
Pretty Polly
Tom Dooley
Reuben Ranzo
Casey Jones
Railroad Bill
John Henry
Clementine
Oh, Susanna
Bill Bailey
Jeanie With the Light
     Brown Hair
Sweet Adeline

Animals
The Blue Tail Fly
The Fox
Froggie Went A-Courtin'
The Old Gray Mare
Stewball
Three Blind Mice
Bingo
Old MacDonald Had a Farm

Play
Camptown Races
Pop Goes the Weasel
Turkey in the Straw
Little Brown Jug
Mountain Dew
What Shall We Do With the
     Drunken Sailor?
A Bicycle Built for Two
For He's A Jolly Good Fellow
This Old Man

---

*The lyrics to all the songs in this list can be found in Irwin and Fred
Silber, The Folksingers Wordbook. New York City: Oak Publications,
1973.

Spirituals & Religious
Sometimes I Feel Like a
          Motherless Child
Michael, Row the Boat Ashore
Study War No More
Just a Closer Walk With Thee
Kum Ba Yah
Nobody Knows the Trouble I've Seen
The Old Gospel Ship
That Old Time Religion
When the Saints Go Marching In
Rock-a-My Soul
Swing Low, Sweet Chariot
Nearer My God To Thee
Rock of Ages
Amazing Grace
We Shall Overcome

Patriotism
The Battle Hymn of the Republic
Yankee Doodle
When Johnny Comes Marching Home

Love--Lost and Found
Black is the Color
The Foggy Dew
My Bonnie Lies Over the
          Ocean
Careless Love
The Cuckoo
On Top of Old Smokey
Wildwood Flower
House of the Rising Sun
Beautiful Brown Eyes
Goodnight Irene
Beautiful Dreamer
St. James Infirmary
In the Good Old Summertime

List #16: Nursery Rhymes

A.   A Sampler of Better-known Nursery Rhymes

1

Humpty Dumpty sat on a wall.
Humpty Dumpty had a great fall.
All the King's horses and all the
    King's men
Couldn't put Humpty together again.

2

There was an old woman who lived
    in a shoe
She had so many children, she didn't
    know what to do.
She gave them some broth without
    any bread,
And whipped them all soundly
    and put them to bed.

3

Yankee doodle went to town
A'riding on a pony.
He put a feather in his cap
And called it macaroni.
Yankee doodle keep it up
Yankee doodle dandy
Mind the music and the step
And with the girls be handy.

4

Hey diddle diddle
The cat and the fiddle
The cow jumped over the moon
The little dog laughed
To see such sport
And the dish ran away with
    the spoon.

5

Old Mother Hubbard
Went to the cupboard
To get her poor dog a bone.
But when she got there
Her cupboard was bare,
And so her poor dog had none.

6

Jack Sprat could eat no fat.
His wife could eat no lean.
And so betwixt the two of them
They licked the platter clean.

7

Peter Piper picked a peck of
    pickled peppers.
A peck of pickled peppers Peter
    Piper picked.
If Peter Piper picked a peck of
    pickled peppers,
Where's the peck of pickled
    peppers Peter Piper picked?

8

She sells sea shells down
    by the sea shore.
The shells she sells are sea
    shore shells.

9

Thirty days hath September,
April, June, and November.
All the rest have thirty-one
Save February which alone
Has 28 and one day more
When Leap Year comes one year
    in four.

10

ABCDEFG, HIJKLMNOP, QRS and TUV
    W and XYZ
Now I've said my ABC's
Tell me what you think of me.

11

Solomon Grundy
Born on Monday
Christened on Tuesday
Married on Wednesday
Sick on Thursday
Worse on Friday
Died on Saturday
Buried on Sunday
That was the end
Of Solomon Grundy.

12

Tweedle-dee and Tweedle-dum
Resolved to have a battle,
For Tweedle-dum said Tweedle-dee
Had spoiled his nice new rattle.
Just then flew by a monstrous crow
As big as a tar barrel,
Which frightened both the heroes so
They quite forgot their quarrel.

13	14
Jack and Jill went up the hill	Needles and pins,
To fetch a pail of water	Needles and pins.
Jack fell down and broke his crown	When a man marries
And Jill came tumbling after.	His trouble begins.

B.   Others

As I was going to St. Ives.

Bah, Bah, black sheep.
Birds of a feather flock together.
Bow, wow, wow, whose dog art thou?
Bye, baby bunting.

Christmas is coming, the goose
    is getting fat.
Cock-a-doodle-doo.
Cock Robin.
Cry, baby, cry.

Diddle, diddle dumpling, my
    son John.
Fie, fi, fo, fum.
For want of a nail.

Georgie Porgie, puddin' and pie.
Goosey, goosey, gander.

Hark, hark, the dogs do bark.
Here we go round the mulberry bush.
Hickery, dickery, dock.
Hot cross buns.
Hush-a-bye, baby, on the tree top.

If wishes were horses.
Jack be nimble, Jack be quick.

Ladybird, ladybird.
Lion and the Unicorn, The
Little Bo-Peep has lost her sheep.
Little Boy Blue, come blow your
    horn.
Little Jack Horner sat in the
    corner.
Little Miss Muffet sat on a tuffet.
Little Nancy Etticoat
Little Polly Flinders
Little Robin Redbreast sat upon a tree.
Little Tommy Tucker.
Little Tommy Tittlemouse.

Mary had a little lamb.
Mistress Mary, quite contrary.

Now I lay me down to sleep.

Old King Cole.
Old Mother Goose.
One misty, misty morning.
One, two, buckle my shoe.

Pat-a-cake, pat-a-cake, baker's man.
Pease porridge hot.
Peter, Peter, pumpkin eater.
Polly put the kettle on.
Pussy cat, pussy cat.

Queen of Hearts, The

Rain, rain, go away.
Ride a cock horse to Banbury Cross
Ring around the roses
Rock-a-bye baby

See-saw, Margory Daw.
Simple Simon met a pieman.
Sing a Song of Sixpence

There was a crooked man.
This is the house that Jack built.
Three little kittens lost their
    mittens.
Tom, Tom, the piper's son.
To market, to market to buy a
    fat pig.

Wee Willie Winkie ran through
    the town.
What are little boys made of?

List #17: American Literature

Note: In this list of authors, we have presented one and occasionally two of the author's better-known works. Needless to say, other authors and other works could have been included in the list. We invite you to add your own favorites.

A.   Noted American Writers of the Past

Louisa May Alcott	1832-1888	Little Women
Sherwood Anderson	1876-1941	Winesburg, Ohio
Stephen Vincent Benet	1898-1943	John Brown's Body
Pearl Buck	1892-1973	The Good Earth
Willa Cather	1876-1947	O Pioneers! My Antonia
James Fenimore Cooper	1789-1851	Leatherstocking Tales
Stephen Crane	1871-1900	The Red Badge of Courage
John Dos Passos	1896-1970	U.S.A.
Theodore Dreiser	1871-1945	An American Tragedy
		Sister Carrie
Ralph Waldo Emerson	1803-1882	Essays
William Faulkner	1897-1962	The Sound and the Fury
Edna Ferber	1885-1968	Showboat
F. Scott Fitzgerald	1896-1940	The Great Gatsby
Robert Frost	1874-1963	"Birches"
Lorraine Hansberry	1930-1965	A Raisin in the Sun
Bret Harte	1836-1902	The Luck of Roaring Camp
Ernest Hemingway	1899-1961	A Farewell to Arms
		For Whom the Bell Tolls
O. Henry (W.S. Porter)	1862-1910	The Gift of the Magi
Langston Hughes	1902-1967	The Weary Blues
Washington Irving	1783-1859	"Rip Van Winkle"
		"The Legend of Sleepy Hollow"
Shirley Jackson	1919-1965	The Lottery
Henry James	1843-1916	The American
Sinclair Lewis	1885-1951	Babbit, Main Street
Jack London	1876-1916	Call of the Wild, Sea Wolf
Henry Wadsworth Longfellow	1807-1882	"Evangeline", "Hiawatha"
Carson McCullers	1917-1967	The Heart is a Lonely Hunter
Herman Melville	1819-1891	Moby Dick, Billy Budd
H.L. Mencken	1880-1956	The American Language
Margaret Mitchell	1900-1949	Gone With the Wind
Ogden Nash	1902-1971	Hard Lines
Clifford Odets	1906-1963	Waiting for Lefty
John O'Hara	1905-1970	Butterfield 8
Eugene O'Neill	1888-1953	Long Day's Journey Into Night
Thomas Paine	1737-1809	Common Sense, The Crisis
Edgar Allen Poe	1809-1849	"The Raven"
Ezra Pound	1885-1972	Cantos
James Whitcomb Riley	1849-1916	"When the Frost is on the Pumpkin"
Edward Arlington Robinson	1869-1935	"Richard Cory"
Carl Sandburg	1878-1967	Chicago Poems
George Santayana	1863-1952	The Sense of Beauty

Upton Sinclair	1878-1968	The Jungle
Gertrude Stein	1874-1946	Three Lives
John Steinbeck	1902-1968	Grapes of Wrath
Wallace Stevens	1879-1955	The Man With the Blue Guitar
Harriet Beecher Stowe	1811-1896	Uncle Tom's Cabin
Booth Tarkington	1869-1946	Seventeen, Penrod
James Thurber	1894-1961	The Owl in the Attic
Mark Twain	1835-1910	The Adventures of Huckleberry Finn
Edith Wharton	1862-1937	Ethan Frome
Walt Whitman	1819-1892	Leaves of Grass
John Greenleaf Whittier	1807-1892	"Snow-bound"
Thornton Wilder	1897-1975	Our Town
William Carlos Williams	1883-1963	Tempers
Edmund Wilson	1895-1972	To the Finland Station
P.G. Woodehouse	1881-1975	Anything Goes
Thomas Wolfe	1900-1938	You Can't Go Home Again

B.   Notable American Writers--Living

Nelson Algren	1909-	The Man With the Golden Arm
James Baldwin	1924-	The Fire Next Time
John Barth	1930-	Giles Goat Boy
Saul Bellow	1915-	Herzog
Ray Bradbury	1920-	Fahrenheit 451
Truman Capote	1924-	In Cold Blood
John Cheever	1912-	The Wapshot Chronicle
James Dickey	1923-	Deliverance
E.L. Doctorow	1931-	Ragtime
Allen Drury	1918-	Advise & Consent
Ralph Ellison	1914-	The Invisible Man
James T. Farrell	1904-	Studs Lonigan
Joseph Heller	1923-	Catch 22
Lilian Hellman	1907-	Pentimento
John Hersey	1914-	A Bell for Adano
Chester Himes	1909-	Cotton Comes to Harlem
Ken Kesey	1935-	One Flew Over the Cuckoo's Nest
Harper Lee	1926-	To Kill a Mockingbird
Norman Mailer	1923-	The Naked and the Dead
Bernard Malamud	1914-	The Fixer
Mary McCarthy	1912-	The Group
James Michener	1907-	Tales of the South Pacific
Arthur Miller	1915-	The Death of a Salesman
Joyce Carol Oates	1938-	Do With Me What You Will
S.J. Perelman	1904-	Ill-Tempered Clavichord
Katherine Ann Porter	1890-	Ship of Fools
Thomas Pynchon	1937-	Gravity's Rainbow
Ayn Rand	1905-	Atlas Shrugged
Philip Roth	1933-	Portnoy's Complaint

J.D. Salinger	1919-	Catcher in the Rye
William Saroyan	1908-	Human Comedy
Neil Simon	1927-	Barefoot in the Park
William Styron	1925-	Confessions of Nat Turner
John Updike	1932-	Rabbit, Run
Kurt Vonnegut, Jr.	1922-	Breakfast of Champions
Robert Penn Warren	1905-	All the King's Men
Tennessee Williams	1911-	A Streetcar Named Desire

List #18: Famous Quotations

Give me liberty or give me death.	Patrick Henry
I have just begun to fight.	John Paul Jones
Don't one of you fire until you see the whites of their eyes.	William Prescott
I never met a man I didn't like. All I know is what I see in the papers.	Will Rogers
You can fool all of the people some of the time and some of the people all of the time, but you can't fool all of the people all of the time.	P.T. Barnum
Ask not what your country can do for you, ask what you can do for your country.	John F. Kennedy
Go West, young man.	Horace Greeley
Make sure you're right, and then go ahead.	Davey Crockett
Win one for the Gipper.	Knute Rockne
Why don't you come up and see me some time.	Mae West
Speak softly and carry a big stick; you will go far.	Theodore Roosevelt
The buck stops here.	Harry S. Truman
It's a small step for a man, but a giant step for mankind.	Neil Armstrong
Play it again, Sam. Here's looking at you, kid.	Humphrey Bogart (Casablanca)
Life begins at forty.	Walter B. Pitkin
If you don't like the weather in New England, just wait a few minutes.	Samuel Clemens (Mark Twain)
I only regret that I have but one life to give for my country.	Nathan Hale
That's all there is, there isn't any more.	Ethel Barrymore
Fifty million Frenchmen can't be wrong.	Texas Guinan
The way to a man's heart is through his stomach.	Sara Payson Willis

What this country needs is a good five-cent
    cigar.   Thomas Riley Marshall

Drive carefully; the life you save may
    be your own.   Highway sign

Nice guys finish last.   Leo Durocher

He can run, but he can't hide.   Joe Louis

You scratch my back and I'll scratch yours.   Simon Cameron

Politics makes strange bedfellows   Charles Dudley Warner

All dressed up, with nowhere to go.   William Allen White

Now is the time for all good men to come
    to the aid of the party.   Charles E. Weller

Hew to the line, let the chips fall where
    they may.   Roscoe Conkling

Taxation without representation is tyranny.   James Otis

Too little and too late   Allan Nevins

Praise the Lord and pass the ammunition.   Howell Maurice Forgy

Hurry up and wait.
Kilroy was here.
That's the way the ball bounces.   Army sayings

I shall return.   Douglas MacArthur

Nuts!   Gen. Anthony McAuliffe

Don't give up the ship.   Capt. James Lawrence

There's a sucker born every minute.   P.T. Barnum

Never give a sucker an even break.   W.C. Fields

I cried all the way to the bank.   Liberace

When you call me that, smile!   Owen Wister

I never forget a face, but in your case
    I'll make an exception.   Groucho Marx

List #19: Proverbs*

The list of proverbs has been correlated with list of Topics (page 69 ff.). Obviously, the assignment of a proverb to a particular semantic category can be done according to several different criteria. We have assigned the proverbs mostly on the basis of their literal rather than figurative meaning.

Food

Half a loaf is better than none.
Variety is the spice of life.
...bread is buttered on both sides.

Cooking

Too many cooks spoil the broth.
The pot calls the kettle black.
Out of the frying pan into the fire.

Eating

Don't bite the hand that feeds you.
Take with a grain of salt.
One man's meat is another man's poison.
You can't eat your cake and have it too.
First come, first served.

Housing/Housekeeping

A woman's work is never done.
Home is where the heart is.
There's no place like home.
People in glass houses shouldn't throw stones.
Walls have ears.

Clothing

He's too big for his breeches.
If the shoe fits, wear it.
A stitch in time saves nine.

*From Dictionary of American Proverbs, David Kin, ed. Philosophical Library.

Human Relationships

Every man for himself.
Like father, like son.
A friend in need is a friend indeed.
Familiarity breeds contempt.
One good turn deserves another.
Live and let live.
It takes one to know one.
Two is company, three is a crowd.
Children should be seen, not heard.
Spare the rod and spoil the child.

Human Qualities & Stages

He who hesitates is lost.
Honesty is the best policy.
Haste makes waste.
Where there's a will, there's a way.
Beauty is only skin-deep.
Beggars can't be choosers.

A sucker is born every minute.
Don't throw out the baby with the bath water.
Boys will be boys.
As the boy is, so is the man.
Never say die.
Dead men tell no tales.

Time

Time heals all wounds.
Never put off till tomorrow what you can do today.
Rome was not built in a day.
Tomorrow never comes.
Better late than never.
Here today, gone tomorrow.
Last but not least.

Weather

Save it for a rainy day.
Make hay while the sun shines.

Geography

Don't make a mountain out of a mole-hill.

Animals

You can't make a silk purse out of a sow's ear.
Don't throw pearls before swine.
His bark is worse than his bite.
Let sleeping dogs lie.
You can't teach an old dog new tricks.
Curiosity killed the cat.
...let the cat out of the bag.
There are many ways to skin a cat.
When the cat's away the mice will play.
You can lead a horse to water, but you can't make him drink.
Don't look a gift horse in the mouth.

Birds

The early bird catches the worm.
Kill two birds with one stone.
A bird in the hand is worth two in the bush.
Birds of a feather flock together.
Don't count your chickens before they hatch.

Plants & Trees

...can't see the forest for the trees.

Language

Hear no evil, see no evil, speak no evil.
A word to the wise is sufficient.
Easier said than done.
No sooner said than done.
Ask me no questions and I'll tell you no lies.
Actions speak louder than words.
Put up or shut up.

Thinking

Seeing is believing.
Out of sight, out of mind.
Necessity is the mother of invention.
Let your conscience be your guide.
Two heads are better than one.

Numbers

Six of one and half-a-dozen of another.
Give him an inch and he'll take a mile.
When angry, count to ten.

Substances and Materials

A rolling stone gathers no moss.
All that glitters is not gold.
You never miss the water 'till the well runs dry.
Good riddance to bad rubbish.
Every little bit helps.

Containers

Don't put all your eggs in one basket.
One rotten apple spoils the barrel.

Emotions

Love makes the world go 'round.
Absence makes the heart grow fonder.
It's no use crying over spilled milk.
Better safe than sorry.
Misery loves company.
Once bitten, twice shy.
We have nothing to fear but fear itself.
He who laughs last, laughs best.

The Body & Its Functions

Cold hands, warm heart.
The way to a man's heart is through his stomach.
In one ear and out the other.
Don't cut off your nose to spite your face.
Blood is thicker than water.
Look before you leap.

Transportation

Don't put the cart before the horse.
It's like carrying coals to Newcastle.

Money

Money doesn't grow on trees.
Money talks.
Money is the root of all evil.
Money burns a hole in the pocket.
Don't throw good money after bad.
A penny saved is a penny earned.
The best things in life are free.
Easy come, easy go.

Recreation

All work and no play makes Jack a dull boy.
The more the merrier.

Sports and Games

Slow and steady wins the race.
Turn about is fair play.
The bigger they come, the harder they fall.
Sink or swim.
If you can't beat 'em, join 'em.
Practice makes perfect.

Medicine and Health

An apple a day keeps the doctor away.
An ounce of prevention is worth a pound of cure.

Business

Nothing ventured, nothing gained.
Never give a sucker an even break.
Every man has his price.
Business before pleasure.
The customer is always right.

Shops and Tools

Jack of all trades, master of none.
A bad workman blames his tools.
...hit the nail on the head.
A chain is as strong as its weakest link.
Don't saw off the branch you're sitting on.

Law

Truth will out.
Two wrongs don't make a right.
The end justifies the means.

Government & Politics

United we stand, divided we fall.

Media

Bad news travels fast.
No news is good news.
The pen is mightier than the sword.
Don't judge a book by its cover.

Education

Practice what you preach.
Do as I say, not as I do.

War

Don't give up the ship.
All is fair in love and war.

Energy

Where there's smoke, there's fire.
...burn the candle at both ends.

List #20: Superstitions

1.   The ACE OF SPADES is a sign of death.

2.   To get out of BED on the wrong side means you will have a bad day.

3.   It is unlucky to have a BLACK CAT cross the road in front of you.

4.   The BRIDE should not see the husband on the morning before the wedding.

5.   The BRIDE should be carried across the doorstop.

6.   CATTLE lying down indicate rain.

7.   A four-leaf CLOVER brings good luck.

8.   A CRICKET in the house is good luck.

9.   A HORSESHOE nailed over the door brings good luck.

10. To pass under a LADDER brings bad luck.

11. It is bad luck to kill a LADYBIRD beetle.

12. LIGHTNING never strikes twice in the same place.

13. Lighting three cigarettes from one MATCH brings bad luck (or pregnancy) to the third person.

14. To break a MIRROR brings seven year's bad luck.

15. Finding a PIN (or a PENNY) brings good luck "See a pin and pick it up; all the day you'll have good luck."

16. Carrying a RABBIT'S FOOT brings good luck.

17. There is a pot of gold at the end of a RAINBOW.

18. If you spill the SALT, throw it over your shoulder.

19. SNAKES never die until sundown.

20. To kill a SPIDER brings rain.

21. Make a wish on a falling STAR.

22. Handling TOADS will cause warts.

23   Opening an UMBRELLA in the house is bad luck.

List #21: Curses and Oaths

A. Mild Words and Phrases

cripes	golly	gol dang it
dang	gosh	darn it all
darn	heck	for crying out loud
tarnation	shoot	what in tarnation
frigging	shucks	son of a gun
fudge	sugar	go fly a kite
gee	geez	

B. Dangerous Words and Phrases*

asshole	fool	damn it (all)
bastard	fuck	eat it
bitch	God	fuck you
Christ	hell	give a shit
cocksucker	jerk	go fuck yourself
crap	queer	go to hell
creep	screw	God damn it
damn	shit	Jesus Christ
fag	turkey	Jesus H. Christ
fairy	witch	piss off
		pissed off
		screw you
		shove it
		sit on it
		son of a bitch
		stick it up your ass
		up yours

*A word of caution is in order. This list is included for the purpose
of comprehension. It is ill-advised to attempt to use these curses
and oaths until one is thoroughly acculturated. The words in this list
are not all equally offensive, but they are all potentially dangerous
if not used properly.

List #22: Names

Common Given Names

A.   Names of women.

Alice	Elizabeth	Laura
Alison	Bess	Lillian
Amanda	Beth	Linda
Mandy	Betsy	Louisa
Andrea	Betty	Lucy
Angela	Libby	Mabel
Ann	Lizzy	Margaret
Anne	Ellen	Meg
Anna	Emily	Maggie
Anita	Evelyn	Mary
Annette	Faith	Maria
Barbara	Fay	Marianne
Beatrice	Frances	Marion
Belle	Gail	May
Blanche	Georgia	Marilyn
Brenda	Gloria	Marjory
Candice	Grace	Margie
Candy	Hannah	Martha
Carol	Helen	Marty
Caroline	Isabel	Nancy
Carolyn	Jaqueline	Patricia
Carrie	Jackie	Patty
Catherine	Jane	Pat
Cathy	Janet	Paula
Kate	Janice	Peggy
Kay	Jean	Penny
Kitty	Jeannette	Polly
Cathleen	Jennifer	Rebecca
Christina	Jenny	Becky
Christine	Jill	Ruth
Christie	Joan	Sally
Clara	Joanna	Sandy
Clare	Josephine	Sophia
Daisy	Joy	Susan
Deborah	Judith	Suzanne
Debbie	Judy	Susie
Diana	Julia	Sue
Donna	Julie	Terry
Doris	June	Vicky
Edith	Karen	Virginia
Eileen		Ginny
Eleanor		
Ella		
Ellie		
Nell		

B.   Names of Men

Albert	Francis	Mark
Alexander	Frank	Matthew
Alfred	Frederic	Michael
Allan	Fred	Mike
Al	Gene	Oliver
Andrew	George	Patrick
Andy	Gerald	Pat
Anthony	Gus	Paul
Tony	Guy	Peter
Arthur	Hal	Pete
Art	Hank	Ralph
Barry	Harold	Raymond
Benjamin	Henry	Ray
Ben	Howard	Richard
Bert	James	Dick
Bill	Jim	Robert
Billy	Jerry	Bob
Bob	John	Roger
Bobby	Jack	Ronald
Brian	Joseph	Ron
Bruce	Joe	Roy
Carl	Keith	Samuel
Charles	Kenneth	Sam
Charlie	Ken	Sandy
Christopher	Lawrence	Saul
Chris	Larry	Scott
Daniel	Leonard	Stanley
Dan	Leroy	Stan
David	Louis	Steven
Dave	Lou	Stephen
Dennis		Steve
Donald		Stewart
Don		Stu
Douglas		Ted
Doug		Thomas
Edgar		Tom
Edward		Timothy
Ed		Tim
Eric		Victor
Ernest		Vic
Ernie		Walter
		Wally
		Walt
		William
		Will
		Bill

C. Most Common Family Names

Rank	Surname	No. of Persons
1	Smith	2,382,500
2	Johnson	1,807,300
3	Williams(on)	1,568,900
4	Brown	1,362,900
5	Jones	1,331,200
6	Miller	1,131,900
7	Davis	1,047,800
8	Martin(ez)	1,046,300
9	Anderson	825,600
10	Wilson	787,800
11	Harris(on)	754,100
12	Taylor	696,000
13	Moore	693,300
14	Thomas	688,100
15	White	636,200
16	Thompson	635,400
17	Jackson	630,000
18	Clark	549,100
19	Roberts(on)	524,700
20	Lewis	495,000
21	Walker	486,500
22	Robins(on)	485,000
23	Peters(on)	479,200
24	Hall	471,500
25	Allen	458,400

Source: U.S. Social Security Administration. Adapted from The
Hammond Almanac. Maplewood, N.J. 1981.

List #23: Place Names

A.   Common Place Names

Washington	Troy	Fairfield
Jefferson	Hanover	Longmeadow
Madison	Salem	Wheaton
Monroe	Stratford	Richmond
Jackson	London	Hampton
Lincoln	Springfield	Pleasantville
Franklin	Greenfield	Dover
Lafayette	Evanston	Plymouth
Leesburg	Guilford	Bloomington
Libertyville	New Haven	Summerville
Independence	Edgewood	Brookfield
Columbia	Riverdale	Highland Park
Lexington	Elkton	Portland
Lebanon	Deerfield	Newport
Canton	Elmwood	Princeton

B.   English elements of common place names*

North -	-town	- City
East -	-ton	- Village
South -	-ville	- Park
West -	-apolis	- Valley
New -	-ford	- Junction
Fort -	-lands	- Hills
Brook -	-wood	- Mills
Saint -	-forest	- Locks
Mount -	-crest	- Lake
Great -	-port	- Beach
Little -	-side	- Point
Oak -	-field	- Haven
Elm -	-bridge	- Harbor
Pine -	-burg	- Shores
Maple -	-bury	- Rock
Cedar -	-boro(ugh)	- Bluffs
Port -	-minster	- Rapids
Glen -	-stead	- Heights
	-view	- Springs
	-vale	- Falls
	-dale	- Creek
	-sex	- Ferry

*Indian, Spanish, and French place names are also common, e.g., Chicago, Mississippi, Santa Fe, San Francisco, New Orleans, Vermont. However, the practice of building place names from standard elements prefixed and/or suffixed to family names is typically English, e.g., East Hartford Junction.

List #24:   Religions

Major Religions

Membership in round figures*

Roman Catholic	50,000,000
Baptist	15,000,000
Methodist	13,000,000
Lutheran	10,000,000
Presbyterian	3,725,000
Episcopal	2,800,000
Mormon	2,600,000
Church of Christ	2,500,000
Greek Orthodox	2,000,000
Muslim	2,000,000
Jewish	1,850,000
United Church of Christ	1,800,000
Pentecostal	1,400,000
Disciples of Christ	1,250,000
Christian Churches and Churches of Christ	1,000,000
Orthodox Church in America	1,000,000
Jehovah's Witness	550,000
Seventh Day Advent	525,000
Armenian Church of America	500,000

*Source: 1980 World Almanac and Book of Facts

List #25: Sports Teams

BASKETBALL

NBA: National Basketball Association

Atlanta Hawks	Indiana Pacers	Phoenix Suns
Boston Celtics	Kansas City Kings	Portland Trailblazers
Chicago Bulls	Los Angeles Lakers	San Antonio Spurs
Cleveland Cavaliers	Milwaukee Bucks	San Diego Clippers
Denver Nuggets	New Jersey Nets	Seattle Super Sonics
Detroit Pistons	New York Knickerbockers	Utah Jazz
Golden State Warriors	Philadelphia 76ers	Washington Bullets
Houston Rockets		

BASEBALL

American League

Baltimore Orioles	Detroit Tigers	Oakland A's
Boston Red Sox	Kansas City Royals	Seattle Mariners
California Angels	Milwaukee Brewers	Texas Rangers
Chicago White Sox	Minnesota Twins	Toronto Blue Jays
Cleveland Indians	New York Yankees	

National League

Atlanta Braves	Los Angeles Dodgers	Pittsburgh Pirates
Chicago Cubs	Montreal Expos	St. Louis Cardinals
Cincinnati Reds	New York Mets	San Diego Padres
Houston Astros	Philadelphia Phillies	San Francisco Giants

HOCKEY

NHL: National Hockey League

Atlanta Flames	Hartford Whalers	Pittsburgh Penguins
Boston Bruins	Los Angeles Kings	Quebec Nordiques
Buffalo Sabres	Minnesota North Stars	St. Louis Blues
Chicago Blackhawks	Montreal Canadiens	Toronto Maple Leafs
Colorado Rockies	New York Islanders	Vancouver Canucks
Detroit Red Wings	New York Rangers	Washington Capitals
Edmonton Oilers	Philadelphia Flyers	Winnipeg Jets

FOOTBALL

NFL: National Football League

Atlanta Falcons	Houston Oilers	Oakland Raiders
Baltimore Colts	Kansas City Chiefs	Philadelphia Eagles
Buffalo Bills	Los Angeles Rams	Pittsburgh Steelers
Chicago Bears	Miami Dolphins	St. Louis Cardinals
Cincinnati Bengals	Minnesota Vikings	San Diego Chargers
Cleveland Browns	New England Patriots	San Francisco 49ers
Dallas Cowboys	New Orleans Saints	Seattle Seahawks
Denver Broncos	New York Giants	Tampa Bay Buccaneers
Detroit Lions	New York Jets	Washington Redskins
Green Bay Packers		

SOCCER

NASL: North American Soccer League

Atlanta Chiefs	Los Angeles Aztecs	San Diego Sockers
California Surf	Memphis Rogues	San Jose Earthquakes
Chicago Sting	Minnesota Kicks	Seattle Sounders
Dallas Tornado	New England Tea Men	Tampa Bay Rowdies
Detroit Express	New York Cosmos	Toronto Blizzard
Edmonton Drillers	Philadelphia Fury	Tulsa Roughnecks
Ft. Lauderdale Strikers	Portland Timbers	Vancouver Whitecaps
Houston Hurricane	Rochester Lancers	Washington Diplomats

List #26:   Sports Personalities

BASEBALL

Hank Aaron	(1934-)	Mickey Mantle	(1931-)
Cool Papa Bell	(1903-)	Willie Mays	(1931-)
Rod Carew	(1945-)	Stan Musial	(1920-)
Ty Cobb	(1886-1961)	Mel Ott	(1909-1958)
Dizzy Dean	(1911-1974)	Satchel Paige	(1906-)
Joe DiMaggio	(1914-)	Jackie Robinson	(1919-1972)
Leo Durocher	(1906-)	Babe Ruth	(1895-1948)
Bob Feller	(1918-)	Warren Spahn	(1921-)
Lou Gehrig	(1903-1941)	Casey Stengel	(1895-1975)
Josh Gibson	(1911-1947)	Honus Wagner	(1874-1955)
Lefty Grove	(1900-1975)	Ted Williams	(1918-)
Rogers Hornsby	(1896-1963)	Cy Young	(1867-1955)
Sandy Koufax	(1935-)		

BASKETBALL

Kareem Abdul Jabbar	(1947-)	George Mikan	(1924-)
Elgin Baylor	(1934-)	Bob Petit	(1932-)
Wilt Chamberlin	(1936-)	Oscar Robertson	(1938-)
Bob Cousy	(1928-)	Bill Russell	(1934-)
John Havlicek	(1940-)	Jerry West	(1938-)

BOXING

Muhammad Ali	(1942-)	Floyd Patterson	(1935-)
James J. Corbett	(1866-1933)	Sugar Ray Robinson	(1920-)
Jack Dempsey	(1895-)	John L. Sullivan	(1858-1918)
Joe Frazier	(1944-)	Gene Tunney	(1897-)
Joe Louis	(1914-)	Joe Walcott	(1914-)
Rocky Marciano	(1923-1969)	Mickey Walker	(1901-)
Archie Moore	(1913-)		

FOOTBALL

George Blanda	(1927-)	Knute Rockne	(1883-1931)
Jim Brown	(1936-)	Amos Alonzo Stagg	(1862-1965)
Otto Graham	(1921-)	Bart Starr	(1934-)
Red Grange	(1903-)	Fran Tarkenton	(1940-)
Bronco Nagurski	(1908-)	Johnny Unitas	(1933-)

GOLF

Patty Berg	(1918-)	Jack Nicklaus	(1940-)
Julius Boros	(1920-)	Arnold Palmer	(1929-)
Billy Casper	(1931-)	Gene Sarazen	(1902-)
Walter Hagen	(1892-)	Sam Snead	(1912-)
Ben Hogan	(1912-)	Kathy Whitworth	(1939-)
Bobby Jones	(1902-1971)	Mickey Wright	(1935-)
Byron Nelson	(1912-)		

SWIMMING

Mark Spitz	(1950-)	Johnny Weismuller	(1903-)

TENNIS

Arthur Ashe	(1943-)	Althea Gibson	(1927-)
Don Budge	(1915-)	Billie Jean King	(1943-)
Maria Bueno	(1939-)	Jack Kramer	(1921-)
Maureen Connelly	(1934-1969)	Alice Marble	(1913-)
Jimmy Connors	(1952-)	Bill Tilden	(1893-1953)
Chris Evert	(1954-)	Helen Wills	(1906-)
Pancho Gonzalez	(1928-)		

TRACK & FIELD

Bob Beamon	(1946-)	Jesse Owens	(1913-1980)
Dick Fosbury	(1947-)	Wilma Rudolph	(1940-)
Bruce Jenner	(1949-)	Jim Ryun	(1947-)
Rafer Johnson	(1935-)	Wyomia Tyus	(1945-)
Al Oerter	(1936-)	Jim Thorpe	(1888-1953)
Bob Mathias	(1930-)	Babe Didrikson Zaharias	(1914-1956)

List #27: The American School System

Name of School	Grade	Age of Students	Subjects		
Nursery		4	Games, songs, creative playing		
Kindergarten	K	5	Games, drawing, crafts, beginning reading & writing		
Primary or Elementary	1	6	Reading, writing, spelling, adding, drawing, singing		
	2	7	Language arts, subtraction, spelling, drawing, singing		
	3	8	Language arts, social studies, multiplication		
	4	9	Language arts, social studies, division		
	5	10	Language arts, history, geography, fractions		
	6	11	Language arts, history, geography, decimals, science		
Junior High	7	12	Language arts, history, geograhpy, algebra, science, foreign language, manual arts, home economics		
	8	13	Language arts, history, geography, geometry, science, foreign language, manual arts, home economics		
High School	9 Freshman 10 Sophomore 11 Junior 12 Senior	14 15 16 17	College Prep	Vocational	Business
			English Math Science Physical Biology Physics Chemistry Foreign Lang. Spanish French	English Economics Civics Math Shop Home Economics	English Book- keeping Civics Math Typing

Name of School	Grade	Age of Students	Subjects
Junior College (2 yrs)	Freshman	18	English, foreign language, history, biology, physical science, sociology or psychology, physical education, ROTC
	Sophomore	19	
College or University (4 yrs) (under-graduate)	Junior	20	Courses in major and minor fields
	Senior	21	
Graduate or Profes-sional School	MA	22-	One-year plus thesis
	PhD		Three years plus dissertation

List #28:   Television Programming

MORNING	News Programs/Weather Reports Daytime Talk Shows Game Shows/Quiz Programs Daytime Dramas/Soap Operas Cartoons (Saturday) Religious Programs (Sunday) Educational Programs (ETV)
AFTERNOON	Noontime News/Weather/Sports Daytime Talk Shows Soap Operas Afternoon Movies Game Shows Documentaries Children's Programs Sports Programs (Saturday/Sunday)
EVENING	Evening News/Weather/Sports Situation Comedies Mystery Drama Programs Variety Shows Movies Documentaries Special Reports
LATE NIGHT	Nightly News Programs Talk Shows Late Show/Movies

List #29:   American Magazines*

Rank		Circulation (nearest 1,000)
1	TV-Guide	19,043,000
2	Reader's Digest	17,889,000
3	National Geographic	10,414,000
4	Better Homes & Gardens	8,098,000
5	Family Circle	7,754,000
6	Woman's Day	7,560,000
7	McCall's	6,527,000
8	Ladies Home Journal	5,502,000
9	Good Housekeeping	5,271,000
10	Playboy	5,249,000
11	National Enquirer	5,024,000
12	Penthouse	4,712,000
13	Redbook	4,304,000
14	Time	4,273,000
15	The Star	3,292,000
16	Newsweek	2,935,000
17	Cosmopolitan	2,747,000
18	American Legion	2,592,000
19	Sports Illustrated	2,275,000
20	People	2,264,000
21	U.S. News and World Report	2,043,000
22	Field and Stream	2,021,000
23	Glamour	1,879,000
24	Southern Living	1,863,000
25	V.F.W. Magazine	1,829,000

*Source: Magazine Publisher's Association, Inc.

#30: National Anthem

First Verse:

Oh, say can you see by the dawn's early light
    What so proudly we hailed at the twilight's last gleaming?
Whose broad stripes and bright stars through the perilous fight,
    O'er the ramparts we watched were so gallantly streaming?
And the rocket's red glare, the bombs bursting in air,
    Gave proof through the night that our flag was still there.
Oh, say does that star-spangled banner yet wave
    O'er the land of the free and the home of the brave?

#31: The Pledge of Allegiance

I pledge allegiance to the flag of the United States of America
and to the republic for which it stands, one nation under God,
indivisible, with liberty and justice for all.

```
┌─────────────────────────────────┐
│  ┌───────────────────────────┐  │
│  │                           │  │
│  │          THE              │  │
│  │                           │  │
│  │     METALINGUISTIC        │  │
│  │                           │  │
│  │          AND              │  │
│  │                           │  │
│  │     MISCELLANEOUS         │  │
│  │                           │  │
│  │        ASPECTS            │  │
│  │                           │  │
│  └───────────────────────────┘  │
└─────────────────────────────────┘
```

Checklist

___ 1. Glossary of Grammatical Terms

___ 2. Three Phonetic Alphabets

___ 3. A Brief Guide to Punctuation

___ 4. Useful Spelling Rules

___ 5. Differences Between British and American Spelling

___ 6. Some British-American Vocabulary Differences

___ 7. 750 High-Frequency Words

___ 8. Measurement Terms

___ 9. Common Symbols

___ 10. Common Elements

___ 11. Abbreviations

___ 12. Road Signs

___ 13. Roman Numerals

___ 14. Proofreading/Correction Marks

List #1: Glossary of Grammatical Terms

Absolute Construction
A word or phrase which modifies the sentence as a whole, not any single element in it.

The game over, the players left the field.
The cattle having been branded, the cowboys saddled up and rode off.

Active
See Voice.

Adjective
A word which modifies a noun or a pronoun.

The old man walked across that narrow street.

Adjective Clause
A dependent clause serving an adjective function. See Relative Clause.

The woman who performed lives next door to me.

Adjective Phrase
A word or a group of words that functions as an adjective.

dull, exceedingly dull, so very dull, the men who are dull

Adverb
A word which modifies a verb, an adjective, or another adverb.

The car moved slowly in the very heavy traffic.

Adverbial
A word or a group of words which function as adverbs.

He works in a large university.
It rained very hard.
He was happy when his friend arrived.

Adverbial Clause
A dependent clause serving an adverb function. Common adverbial clauses include:

comparison (as...as, as...than)
I can't run as fast as I used to.

concession (though, although, even if...)
Although I had a good time, I was happy to leave.

condition - See Conditional Sentences.

purpose (so as to, in order to, so that, in order that)
We are going to France to learn French.

Adverbial Clause (cont'd.)	reason (because, as, since....) They turned on the lights <u>because it was too dark.</u> result (so...that, such...that) He spoke <u>so fast that no one understood a thing</u>. time (when, as, while, until, as soon as....) <u>As soon as he lit his cigar</u>, people began to leave the room.
Agreement	Correspondence between grammatically related elements. Agreement in number and person between a subject and its verb. (The <u>children</u> <u>play</u>. The <u>child</u> <u>plays</u>.) Agreement in gender, number and person between a pronoun and its antecedent. (The <u>girl</u> washed <u>her</u> face.)
Antecedent	The word to which a pronoun refers. <u>Aunt Mary</u> fainted when <u>she</u> heard the news.
Appositive	A word, phrase, or clause used as a noun and placed next to another noun to modify it. George Washington, <u>the president</u>, slept here.
Article	<u>A</u> and <u>an</u> are indefinite articles. <u>The</u> is the definite article.
Auxiliary	Functional verbs which help other verbs indicate tense, mood, or voice (<u>be</u>, <u>do</u>, <u>have</u>, <u>go</u>). Modal auxiliaries (<u>can</u>, <u>may</u>, <u>might</u>, <u>must</u>, <u>should</u>, etc.) serve also as structural signals and have a meaning of their own (ability, obligation, possibility).
Case	English has remnants of three cases: <u>subjunctive</u>, <u>possessive</u>, and <u>objective</u>. Nouns are inflected for case in the possessive (John's). Some pronouns and the relative pronoun <u>who</u> are inflected <u>subjective</u>: I, he, she, we, they, who; <u>possessive</u>: my (mine), your (yours), his, her (hers), its, our (ours), their (theirs), whose; <u>objective</u>: me, him, her, us, them, whom).
Clause	A group of words containing a subject and a predicate. See Independent Clause and Dependent Clause.
Collective Noun	A noun singular in appearance which indicates a class or a group of persons or things. (a <u>committee</u> of citizens, an <u>army</u>)

Comparative | The form of adjectives and adverbs which is used to indicate relative superiority.

tall	taller	less tall
important	more important	less important
slowly	more slowly	less slowly

Complement | A word or group of words used to complete a predicate. Predicate nominatives, predicate adjectives, direct objects, and indirect objects are complements.

Compound Sentence | A sentence which combines two or more independent clauses.

He whistled, and she worked.

Complex Sentence | A sentence which contains one or more dependent clauses.

He whistled while she worked.

Compound-Complex Sentence | A sentence which contains two or more independent clauses and one or more dependent clauses.

He whistled and she worked until they both got tired.

Conditional Sentences | Conditional sentences have two parts, the conditional clause and the main clause. There are three types:

1) Real condition:
If you bother the cat, it will scratch you.

2) Unreal, contrary-to-fact condition (present):
If I were you, I would keep the money.
If you took a trip, where would you go?

3) Unreal, contrary-to-fact condition (past):
If I had known you were coming, I would have
baked you a cake.
If I had been Lincoln, I wouldn't have gone to the
theater that night.

Conjunction | A word used to connect sentences or sentence parts. See also Coordinating Conjunctions, Subordinating Conjunctions.

Connective | See Conjunction.

Conjunctive Adverbs | Adverbs used to relate two independent clauses separated by a semicolon: then, consequently, however, moreover, therefore, etc.

Coordinating Conjunctions	The simple conjunctions that connect sentences and sentence parts of equal rank: and, but, or, nor, for, yet, so.
Correlative Conjunctions	Pairs of conjunctions which join sentence parts: either... or, neither... nor, not only... but also, both...and.
Count-noun	A noun that can be made plural usually by adding -s.
Demonstrative Adjectives and Pronouns	Words used to point out someone or something: this, that, these, those. Also called demonstrative determiners.
Dependent (Subordinate) Clause	A group of words which contains both a subject and a predicate but which does not stand alone as a sentence. A dependent clause always serves a noun, adverb, or adjective function. See Noun Clause, Adjective Clause, Adverbial Clause, Relative Clause.
Determiners	A class of modifiers which includes articles (a, an, the), possessives (my, John's, his), demonstratives (this, that), interrogatives (which, what), indefinite (some, any), numerals, and each, every.
Diphthong	Two vowel sounds joined in one syllable to form one speech sound: out oil I
Direct Object	A noun, pronoun, or other substantive which receives the action of the verb.
	Jack climbed the beanstalk into the sky.
Direct Speech	Repeats the speaker's exact words, enclosing them in quotation marks.
	He said, "I've lost my umbrella."
Elliptical Clause	A clause in which one or more words necessary for the full subject-predicate structure are omitted but "understood."
	The manager admired no one else as much as (he admired) her. "understood"

Expletive	The it or there which serves to fill the subject slot in it is, there is, and there are sentences. It is easy to understand. There is a fly in my soup.
Finite Verb	A verb in the present or past form. E.g., the finite forms of the verb be are is, am, are, was and were. The non-finite forms of be are be, being, and been.
Function Words	Words which establish grammatical relationships within a sentence: articles, auxiliaries, conjunctions, prepositions, pronouns, determiners, intensifiers, interjections.
Future	I will work, etc.
Gender	The quality of nouns and pronouns that determines a choice between masculine, femine, or neuter (he, she, it).
Gerund	See Verbal.
Idiom	An expression that does not conform to general grammatical patterns but is established through usage as the way of conveying a given meaning. hold up, hold down, be beside oneself, kick the bucket
Indefinite Pronouns	Pronouns not pointing out a particular person, thing, or definite quantity. Some, any, each, every, everyone, everybody, nobody, anyone, anybody, one, neither, are among the most common.
Independent Clause	A group of words which contains a subject and a predicate and which can stand alone as a sentence.
Indirect Object	A word which indirectly receives the action of the verb. The witch gave the pretty girl a poisoned apple.
Indirect Speech	Paraphrases the speaker's words. He said he had lost his umbrella.
Infinitive	See Verbal.

Inflection	Changes in the form of words to reflect changes in grammatical relationships: the cabin s; he walk s, she's talk ing, quick est.
Intensifier	Words that modify adjectives or adverbs and express degree: very beautiful, quite young, rather old.
Intensive Pronoun	A reflexive pronoun ending in -self, -selves and used for emphasis. I'd rather do it myself.
Interjection	A word used to exclaim or to express emotion: ah, oh, ouch.
Interrogative Pronouns	Who, whose, whom, what, which, when used in questions.
Intonation	The rising and falling of the pitch of the voice in speech.
Intransitive Verb	A verb which has no direct object. The tide turned at noon.
Linking Verb	A verb which does not express action but links the subject to another word which names or describes it. Be, become, seem, appear, look, are common linking verbs.
Mass Noun (Non-count Noun)	A noun that refers to a quantity and cannot be preceded by a cardinal number (one, two, etc): sugar, milk, hunger.
Modifier	A word, phrase, or clause which limit or describe other sentence elements or the sentence as a whole.
Mood	The classification of verb forms as indicative (plain or factual: I am ready); imperative (request or command: Be ready at six); and subjunctive (hypothetical or contrary to fact: I wish you were ready).
Nominal	Any structure that functions as a noun.
Nominative Case	See Case, subjective.

Non-Restrictive Relative Clause	A clause which provides further information not essential to identification of the subject or complement and is set off usually with commas. John Jones, <u>who spends a lot of money</u>, has many friends.
Noun	A word which names and classifies people, animals, things, ideas. <u>Thomas Jefferson</u> <u>lemon</u> <u>religion</u> <u>alligator</u> <u>Paris</u> <u>worm</u> <u>justice</u> <u>school</u> <u>committee</u>
Noun Clause	A dependent clause serving a nominal function. Everyone agreed <u>that the play was a success</u>.
Noun Phrase	The element in the sentence which functions as subject, object, or complement. <u>The pretty girl standing in the corner</u> is <u>my sister</u>. <u>She and her friends</u> never dance.
Number	Choice of appropriate forms to indicate singular or plural.
Object of a Preposition	Completes the idea of time, position, direction, etc., begun by a preposition. at his <u>desk</u> towards the <u>door</u>
Objective Complement	A complement after the direct object that provides another name for the object or otherwise amplifies it. They elected him <u>president</u>. The war made many women <u>widows</u>. Everyone believed him <u>crazy</u>.
Participle	See Verbal.
Parts of Speech	Noun, pronoun, adjective, adverb, conjunction, interjection, preposition, article.
Passive	See Voice.
Past	<u>I worked</u>, etc.

Phoneme	A basic unit of sound in a language (/i/, /p/, /iy/).
Perfect	I have worked, I had worked, I will have worked, etc.
Person	Choice of the appropriate forms to express the person speaking (first person: I, we; second person: you; third person: he).
Possessive Adjectives	My, your, his, her, its, our, their.
Predicate	The verb in a clause (simple predicate) or the verb and its modifiers, complements, and objects (complete predicate).
Predicate Adjective	An adjective following a linking verb and describing the subject. The flowers look artificial.
Predicate Nominative	A word or group of words which follows a linking verb and identifies the subject. This book is a best-selling science-fiction novel.
Preposition	A connective which joins a noun or a pronoun to the rest of the sentence. A prepositional phrase may serve either an adverb or an adjective function. adjective - Jack is a master of many trades. adverb - The guide led us into the forest.
Present	I work, etc.
Progressive (Continuous Tense)	I am working, I was working, I have been working, etc.
Pronouns	Words which stand for nouns, classified as: personal (I, you, he, etc.) possessive (my, his, mine, yours) reflexive or intensive (myself, himself, ourselves, etc.) demonstrative (this, that, those, etc.) relative (who, which, what, that, whose) interrogative (who, which, what, etc.) indefinite (one, anyone, everyone)

Quantifiers	Words denoting how much (some, any, most, few, one, two, three, etc.)
Reciprocal Pronouns	Each other, one another.
Relative Clause	A dependent clause related to the main clause by a relative pronoun. The book that he recommended is on sale.
Restrictive Relative Clause	A clause that contributes to the identification of the noun it modifies, not separated by a comma from that noun. See Non-Restrictive Relative Clause. The man who called me up was a complete stranger.
Sentence	A grammatically complete unit of thought or expression, containing at least a subject and a predicate.
Simple Sentence	A sentence consisting of only one independent clause.
Stress	Pronouncing a syllable or a word in such a way that makes it more prominent in a word or sentence respectively. condúctor Let's gó.
Substantive	See Nominal.
Subject	A word or group of words about which the sentence or clause makes a statement. The dog jumped into the car.
Subjective Complement	See Predicate Nominative; Predicate Adjective.
Subjunctive	See Mood.
Subordinating Conjunctions	Conjunctions which join sentence parts of unequal rank. Usually they begin dependent clauses. Some of the most common ones are because, since, though, although, if, when, while, before, after, as, until, so that, as long as, as if, where, unless, as soon as, whereas, in order that.

Superlative   The form of adjectives and adverbs used to express
                      absolute superiority.

                      tall   the tallest   the least tall
                      important   the most important the least important
                      slowly   the most slowly   the least slowly

Syntax   The rules of sentence formation.

Tag Questions   Short yes/no questions added to statements.

                      It's a beautiful day, isn't it?
                      You haven't seen the film, have you?

Tense   The system of verb forms expressing primarily
                      different relationships in time.

Transitive Verb   A verb which normally requires an object.

                      Monkeys love bananas.

Two-Word Verbs   A combination of verb and a preposition or an ad-
                      verb which forms a new vocabulary item. Two-
                      part verbs are classified as intransitive, separable,
                      and non-separable.

                      intransitive: John got up early this morning.
                      separable: John calls up his wife from the
                                       office.
                                     John calls his wife up from the
                                       office.
                                     John calls her up from the office.
                      non-separable: Everybody picks on fat people.

Verb   A word or group of words expressing action,
                      being, or state of being.

                      I swallowed a fly.
                      What is man?
                      The table has been set.

Verbal   A word or phrase derived from a verb and used
                      as a noun, an adjective, or an adverb. Verbals
                      consist of infinitives, gerunds or participles.

                      infinitive: begins with to (sometimes under-
                                     stood) and is used as a noun, an
                                     adverb or an adjective.
                      - noun: To do such a thing would be dis-
                                     astrous.

Verbal (cont'd.)	- adverb:	Many people jog <u>to keep physically fit</u>.
	- adjective:	I'm ready <u>to testify</u>, your Honor.
	<u>gerund</u>:	ends in <u>-ing</u> and is used as a noun.
		<u>Playing with matches</u> is a favorite past-time among children.
	<u>parti-ciple</u>:	ends in <u>-ing</u>, <u>-ed</u>, and is used as an adjective.
		I can't live without <u>running</u> water. <u>Accompanied by his faithful dog</u>, Daniel roamed the woods.

Verb Phrase   Consists of the main verb and one or more auxiliaries.

It <u>is beginning</u> to rain.
It <u>has been raining</u> for a long time.

Modern grammarians use the term <u>verb phrase</u> to indicate the verb and all that goes with it (predicate) or the verb and its modifiers.

The old man and the boy <u>had quietly taken the book from the library</u>.

Voice   A distinction in verb forms between <u>active</u> (the subject is acting) and <u>passive</u> (the subject is acted upon).

<u>active</u>:   Elmer <u>fed</u> the chickens.
<u>passive</u>:   The chickens <u>were fed</u> by Elmer.

List #2: A Comparison of Three Phonetic Alphabets

Consonants   (Symbols follow the I.P.A.; exceptions are indicated.)

Sounds   Representations

	I.P.A.*	T.S.**	Dict.***
may	/ m /		
bay	/ b /		
pay	/ p /		
way	/ w /		
whey	/ ʍ /		/ hw /
vee	/ v /		
fee	/ f /		
thee	/ ð /		/ th /
thigh	/ θ /		/ th /
new	/ n /		
dew	/ d /		
too	/ t /		
Lou	/ l /		
zoo	/ z /		
Sue	/ s /		
you	/ j /	/ y /	/ y /
rue	/ r /		
measure	/ ʒ /	/ ž /	/ zh /
show	/ ʃ /	/ š /	/ sh /
joke	/ dʒ /	/ ǰ /	/ j /
choo	/ tʃ /	/ č /	/ ch /
bang	/ ŋ /		
bag	/ g /		
back	/ k /		
hi	/ h /		

*International Phonetic Alphabet
**Trager-Smith System
***Merriam-Webster dictionary

Vowels   (All vowel sounds in each system are represented.)

Sounds	I.P.A.	T.S.	Dict.
beat	/ i /	/ iy /	/ ē /
bit	/ ɪ /	/ i /	/ i /
bait	/ e /	/ ey /	/ ā /
bet	/ ɛ /	/ e /	/ e /
bat	/ æ /	/ æ /	/ a /
but	/ ʌ /	/ ə /	/ ə /
alone	/ ə /	/ ə /	/ ə /
boot	/ u /	/ uw /	/ ü /
put	/ ʊ /	/ u /	/ u̇ /
boat	/ o /	/ ow /	/ ō /
bought	/ ɔ /	/ ɔ /	/ ȯ /
father	/ a /	/ a /	/ ä /
how	/ aw /	/aw/ /æw/	/ au̇ /
I	/ aj /	/ ay /	/ ī /
boy	/ ɔi /	/ oy /	/ ȯi /
ear		/ ir /	
air		/ er /	
marry		/ ær /	
father		/ ər /	
fur		/ ər /	/ ər /
poor		/ ur /	
or		/ or /	
are		/ ar /	

List #3: A Brief Guide to Punctuation

Apostrophe '

Use an apostrophe
-to indicate omissions in contractions   doesn't, won't
-to indicate possession   Mary's, p's and q's

Brackets ( )

Use brackets
-to indicate comment or question   "He [Lincoln] was assassinated
 in quoted material, or . . .   by a mad actor."
-within parentheses   (Allende killed himself [was
                                        assassinated?] in 1975.)

Colon :

Use a colon
-in writing clock time   9:25   12:01
-to introduce a list   We need the following items:
                                       soap, toothpaste & hand lotion.
-after the names of speakers   The speaker observed: "Four
 in a dialogue   score and twenty years ago..."
-after salutations in formal   Dear Sir:
 or business letters   Dear Mr. Landsdowne:

Comma ,

Use a comma
-after yes or no in a response   Yes, we have bananas.
-before the conjunction in a   The oldest boy is going to
 compound sentence   school, and the youngest is
                                       going to work.
-to separate elements in   New Orleans, Louisiana
 addresses
-to separate equivalent   The barn was dark, warm,
 elements in a series   and damp.
-to separate a speaker's words   John asked, "May I leave?"
 from the introductory statement
-to group large numbers into   9,121   1,268,421
 thousands
-to set off addressee in   "Mary, take this ring."
 direct speech.
-to separate an introductory   When the party was over, I
 clause from the sentence   went home.
-after a mild exclamation   Well, I don't care.
-before/after an appositive   George, a famous poet, spoke.

Comma, (cont'd.)

-to separate a tag question
from the rest of the sentence

It's cold, isn't it?

-before and after a non-
restrictive adjective clause

Punctuation, which is essential
for writing, seems complicated.

Dash —

Use a dash
-to indicate an interruption
or an after-thought

We'll arrive in New York - at
last - in two hours.
I will-at least, I'll try.

-to indicate special emphasis
in place of a comma

Give people what they want -
money, fame, and power.

Exclamation Point !

Use an exclamation point
-to indicate strong feeling
or emotion or for emphasis

Help! Watch out!
She said she'd jump and she
did!

Hyphen —

Use a hyphen
-in certain fixed expressions

person-to-person
matter-of-fact
station-to-station

-in compound numerals

twenty-one   ninety-nine
twenty-first   ninety-ninth
seven-thirty   one-fifteen

-in expressions of clock time
-in joining a prefix to a
proper name

pre-Columbian pre-Roosevelt
un-Christian

-in joining a prefix to a noun
whose first letter is the same
as the last letter of the prefix

anti-intellectual
pre-existing
re-elect

Parentheses ( )

Use parentheses
-to enclose remarks, comments,
explanations, etc. that interrupt the main thought

She invited the two men (they
are cousins) to the party.
If it rains (it usually doesn't),
we'll postpone the picnic.

Period •

Use a period
-at the end of a statement   I want to go home.
-after initials or abbreviations   Mr. P.T. Barnum, 1:00 p.m.
-to indicate cents/decimals $5.50   1.65   .002

Question Mark ?

Use a question mark
-at the end of a direct question   Where does it all end?
-after a tag question   You like to talk, don't you?

Quotation Marks " "

Use quotation marks   "Come here," Jim said.
- to enclose direct quotations   "Hurt Hawks" "I Love Lucy"
- to enclose titles of chapters,   "The Most Dangerous Game"
  articles, songs, TV programs
- with other punctuation as   "Come," he said. "I'm going."
  follows: I said, "I will"; I followed.
                                    "Can you see?" he asked.
                                    Did I answer, "no"?

Semicolon ;

Use a semicolon
-in a compound sentence   The singular form is mouse;
 without a connective   the plural form is mice.
-in a sentence with two main   The teacher was sick; therefore,
 clauses joined by a conjunctive   classes were called off.
 adverb   Mary ran a good race; however,
                                    she failed to qualify for the
                                    finals.

Underlining _____

Underline
-titles of periodicals and books   Newsweek, A Farewell to Arms
-foreign phrases and words   alors   que le vaya bien
 in handwriting or typing
-words emphasized   I wanted three tickets, not four.
-the names of ships, trains   The Titanic   Orient Express
 and airplanes   Constellation

<u>List #4</u>:   Useful <u>Spelling</u> <u>Rules</u>

A.   If a word ends in <u>y</u> preceded by a consonant, change the <u>y</u> to an <u>i</u> before every suffix except <u>-ing</u>.

salary	salaries	copy	copying
marry	married	try	trying
lonely	loneliness	fly	flying
worry	worries	worry	worrying

B.   Write <u>i</u> before <u>e</u>, except after <u>c</u>, or when sounded like <u>a</u>, as in neighbor and weigh.

<u>i</u> before <u>e</u>:	brief, piece, chief, yield
<u>e</u> before <u>i</u>:	receive, deceive, ceiling, freight, sleigh

Exceptions: either, neither, seize, leisure, weird, species, financier

C.   If a word ends with a single consonant preceded by a single vowel (<u>hop</u>, <u>bat</u>) and you add a suffix beginning with a vowel (<u>-er</u>, <u>-ed</u>, <u>-ing</u>), double the final consonant when

the word has only one syllable

stop	stopped	trip	tripped
bat	batter	drop	dropping
rub	rubbing	spin	spinning

the word is accented on the last syllable

occur	occurring	confer	conferred
admit	admitted	omit	omitting

D.   If a word ends with a silent <u>e</u> and you add a suffix,

drop the <u>e</u> if the suffix begins with a vowel

love	lovable	move	moving
desire	desirable	use	usable

keep the <u>e</u> if the suffix begins with a consonant

use	useful	engage	engagement
love	lovely	move	movement

Exceptions: words ending in <u>ee</u> never drop the final <u>ee</u>.

agree	agreement	flee	fleeing

List #5:   Differences Between British and American Spelling

American	British
-e	**-ae**
anesthesia	anaesthesia
encyclopedia	encyclopaedia
-ection	**-exion**
connection	connexion
reflection	reflexion
-ed	**-t**
burned	burnt
learned	learnt
spelled	spelt
-ense	**-ence**
license	licence
defense	defence
-er	**-re**
center	centre
meter	metre
-ization	**-isation**
civilization	civilisation
naturalization	naturalisation
-ize	**-ise**
criticize	criticise
memorize	memorise
-ll	**-l**
fulfill	fulfil
skillful	skilful
-ment	**-ement**
judgment	judgement
argument	arguement
-or	**-our**
color	colour
neighbor	neighbour

Note: <u>In British usage</u>, words ending in an <u>l</u> preceded by a single vowel usually double the <u>l</u>.

| quarrel | quarrelling | model | modelled |
| travel | travelled | signal | signalling |

<u>In American usage</u>, the consonant is doubled only if the last syllable is accented.

| signal | signaling | excel | excellent |
| travel | traveling | propel | propeller |

List #6:   Some American-British Vocabulary Differences*

American	British
aisle (theater)	gangway (theatre)
apartment	flat
baby carriage	perambulator, pram
bar	pub
bartender	barman
bathtub	bath
battery (automobile)	accumulator
bill (money)	banknote
broiled (meat)	grilled
can	tin
candy	sweets
candy store	sweet shop
checkers (game)	draughts
cookie	biscuit
corn	maize
derby (hat)	bowler
detour	diversion
druggist	chemist
elevator	lift
eraser	rubber
faucet	tap
flashlight	torch
french fries	chips
gasoline	petrol
generator	dynamo
groceries	stores
hood (automobile)	bonnet
incorporated (inc.)	limited (ltd.)
installment plan	hire-purchase system

*Adapted from H.L. Mencken, The American Language, Fourth Edition.
New York: Alfred A. Knopf, 1936.

American	British
internal revenue	inland revenue
janitor	caretaker, porter
kerosene	paraffin
kindergarten	infant's school
lawyer	barrister
line	queue
living-room	sitting-room
liquor	spirits
long distance (telephone)	trunk
mailman	postman
oatmeal	porridge
paste	gum
period (punctuation)	full stop
phonograph	gramophone
private school	public school
raincoat	waterproof, mackintosh
rooster	cock
rubbish collector	dustman
second floor	first floor
sedan	saloon car
sidewalk	path
soccer	football
subway	tube
suspenders (men's)	braces
syrup	treacle
taxes	rates
thermos bottle	flask
truck	lorry
vacation	holiday
windshield	windscreen
wrench	spanner

List #7: 750 High-Frequency Words:
A Basic Vocabulary List

Nouns

A   action   afternoon   age   amount   animal   answer   arm   art
     article

B   baby   back   bag   ball   bank   beauty   bed   bird   blood
     boat   body   box   boy   brother   building   business

C   car   (in any) case   cause   center   century   chair   chance
     child(ren)   church   circle   city   class   clothes   cloud
     college   color   company   condition   corner   cost   country
     (of) course   crowd   cup

D   day   date   daughter   deal   death   difference   dinner
     direction   distance   doctor   dog   dollar   door   doubt
     dream   dress   drink

E   ear   earth   east   edge   effort   egg   end   evening   eye

F   face   fact   fall   family   farm   father   favor   fellow   field
     finger   fire   fish   floor   flower   fly   food   foot(feet)
     forest   friend   front   fruit   future

G   game   garden   girl   glass   gold   government   grass   guess

H   hair   hall   hand   hat   head   health   heart   hill   history
     hole   home   horse   hour   house   husband

I   ice   idea   inch   interest   island

J   job   joy

K   kitchen   knee

L   lady   land   law   leg   letter   life   light   line   lip
     (a)lot(of)   love

M   man(men)   matter   meat   meeting   member   middle   mile
     milk   minute   Miss   moment   money   month   moon   morning
     mother   mountain   mouth   music   Mr.   Mrs.

N   name   nation   nature   neck   neighbor   news   night   north
     nose   note   number

O   object   ocean   office   oil   opinion

P   page   pain   pair   pants   paper   part   pastry   past   peace
     people   person   picture   piece   place   plant   pleasure
     pound   power   price   president   problem   public   purpose

Nouns (cont'd.)

Q   quarter   question

R   race   rain   reason   report   result   river   road   rock   room   rule

S   salt   school   sea   season   seat   shade   shape   ship   shoe   shop   shoulder   side   sight   sign   sir   size   skin   sky   snow   song   soul   south   space   spirit   spot   spring   star   stone   storm   story   street   subject   success   sugar   summer   supply   surprise   system

T   table   tear   thing   thought   time   today   tomorrow   top   town   tree   trip   trouble   truth

U   uncle

V   view   voice

W   wall   war   watch   water   way   weather   week   west   wind   window   winter   woman(women)   wood   word

Y   yard   year

Verbs

Irregular (with past forms)

B   be (was, were)   beat (beat)   become (became)   begin (began)   break (broke)   bring (brought)   build (built)   buy (bought)

C   catch (caught)   come (came)   cost (cost)   cut (cut)

D   do (did)   draw (drew)   drink (drank)   drive (drove)

E   eat (ate)

F   fall (fell)   feed (fed)   feel (felt)   fight (fought)   find (found)   fly (flew)   forget (forgot)   forgive (forgave)

G   get (got)   give (gave)   go (went)   grow (grew)

H   hang (hung)   have (had)   hear (heard)   hold (held)   hurt (hurt)

K   keep (kept)   know (knew)

L   lay (laid)   lead (led)   leave (left)   let (let)   lie (lay)   lose (lost)

Irregular Verbs (cont'd.)

M   make (made)   mean (meant)   meet (met)

P   pay (paid)   put (put)

R   read (read)   ride (rode)   rise (rose)   run (ran)

S   say (said)   see (saw)   send (sent)   set (set)   sing (sang)
       sleep (slept)   speak (spoke)   spend (spent)   spread (spread)
       stand (stood)

T   take (took)   teach (taught)   tell (told)   think (thought)

U   understand (understood)

W   wear (wore)   write (wrote)

Regular

A   accept   act   add   admit   agree   allow   appear   arrive   ask

B   belong   believe   burn

C   call   care   carry   change   close   command   consider
       contain   continue   cook   count   cover   cross   cry

D   dance   dare   decide   demand   destroy   discover   doubt
       dream   drop

E   enjoy   enter   escape   expect   explain   express

F   fail   fill   finish   force

H   happen   help   hope   hurry

I   increase   include

J   join

K   kill   kiss

L   laugh   learn   like   listen   live   look   love

M   marry   matter   measure   mind   move

N   need   notice

O   offer   order   open

Regular Verbs (cont'd.)

P   pass   pick   plan   plant   play   point   prepare   promise
     prove   pill

R   rain   reach   realize   remain   remember   reply   return
     ring   run   rush

S   save   serve   share   shout   show   smoke   sound   start
     stay   step   stop   study   suppose

T   talk   taste   thank   touch   travel   try   turn

U   use

W   wait   walk   want   watch   wish   wonder   work

Adjectives

A   able   alone   afraid

B   bad   beautiful   better   best   big   black   blue   (be) born
     bright   brown   bury

C   certain   chief   clean   clear   cold   common   complete   cool

D   dark   dead   deep   different   dry

E   easy

F   fair   famous   fast   fine   foreign   free   fresh   full

G   glad   good   gray   great   green

H   happy   hard   heavy   hot   human   hundred

I   ill   important

L   large   last   late   little   long   low

M   million   modern

N   national   natural   new   next   nice

O   old   only

P   plain   pleasant   poor   possible   pretty

Q   quiet

R   ready   real   red   rich   right   round

Adjectives (cont'd.)

S   safe   several   short   sick   simple   small   soft   special
     square   straight   strong   sure   sweet

T   tall   thin   tired   true

V   various

W   warm   wet   white   whole   wide   wild   wise   wonderful
     wrong

Y   yellow   young

Adverbs

A   again   ago   almost   already   also   always   away

B   before   better   best

C   certainly

E   early   else   especially   even   ever

F   far   finally   forward

H   here   how

I   instead

J   just

M   more

N   nearly   necessary   never   no   not   now

O   often   once   out   outside

P   probably

Q   quickly   quite

R   rather   really

S   so   sometimes   strange   suddenly

T   then   there   today   tomorrow

U   up   usually

Adverbs (cont'd.)

<u>V</u>   very

<u>Y</u>   yes   yet

Conjunctions

<u>A</u>   although   and   as

<u>B</u>   because   both...and   but

<u>E</u>   either...or

<u>H</u>   however

<u>I</u>   if

<u>N</u>   neither...nor

<u>O</u>   or

<u>S</u>   since

<u>T</u>   therefore   though   thus

<u>U</u>   until

<u>W</u>   when   where   whether   while

<u>Y</u>   yet

Prepositions

<u>A</u>   above   about   across   after   against   along   among   around   at

<u>B</u>   behind   beside   between   by

<u>D</u>   down   during

<u>E</u>   except

<u>F</u>   for   from

<u>I</u>   in   into

<u>L</u>   less   like

Prepositions (cont'd.)

<u>O</u>   of   off   on   over

<u>T</u>   through   to   towards

<u>U</u>   under   until   up   upon

<u>W</u>   with   without   within

Pronouns

<u>E</u>   everything

<u>H</u>   he   her   herself   him   himself   his

<u>I</u>   I   it   itself

<u>M</u>   my   myself   mine

<u>N</u>   nothing   none

<u>O</u>   one   other   our   ours

<u>S</u>   she

<u>T</u>   their   them   themselves   they

<u>U</u>   us

<u>W</u>   we   who   whom   whose   what   which

<u>Y</u>   you   your   yourself

Auxiliaries

can   could   may   might   must   ought   shall   should   would

Quantifiers

<u>A</u>   all   any

<u>B</u>   (a little) bit (of)

<u>D</u>   (a great) deal (of)

<u>E</u>   eight   either

Quantifiers (cont'd.)

<u>F</u>   first   five   four

<u>N</u>   neither   nine

<u>O</u>   one

<u>S</u>   second   seven   six

<u>T</u>   third   thirty   thousand   three   twelve   twenty   two

Determiners

<u>A</u>   a   an

<u>E</u>   each   every

<u>T</u>   that   the   these   this   those

<u>W</u>   which   what

List #8: Measurement
(Non-metric)

Linear measure

12 inches   = 1 foot
 3 feet   = 1 yard
5½ yards   = 1 rod
40 rods   = 1 furlong
 8 furlongs = 1 mile

Avoirdupois weight

16 drams   = 1 ounce
16 ounces   = 1 pound
2,000 pounds =   1 ton

Mariner's measure

6 feet   = 1 fathom
1,000 fathoms =   1 nautical mile
3 nautical miles   =   1 league

Liguid measure

2 pints =   1 quart
4 quarts = 1 gallon

Square measure

160 square rods = 1 acre
640 acres   = 1 square mile

Dry measure

2 pints   = 1 quart
8 quarts = 1 peck
4 pecks = 1 bushel

Metric/English Measure Equivalents

1 centimeter (cm.)	=	.3937 inch (in.)
1 meter (m.)	=	39.37 in. or 3.28 feet (ft.)
1 kilometer (km.)	=	.62137 mile (mi.)
1,000 m² = 1 hectacre (ha.)	=	2.471 acres
1 centiliter (cl.)	=	.338 fluid ounces (fl. oz.)
1 liter (l.)	=	.9081 dry quart (qt.)
		1.0567 liquid quarts
1 centigram (cg.)	=	.1543 gram (gr.)
1 gram (g.)	=	15.432 gram (gr.)
		.03527 ounces (oz.)
1 kilogram (kg.)	=	2.2046 pounds (lb.)
1 inch	=	2.54 centimeters
12 in. = 1 foot	=	.3048 meters
3 ft. = 1 yard	=	.9144 meters
16½ ft. = 1 rod	=	5.029 meters
5,280 ft. = 1 mile	=	1.6093 kilometers
4,840 yd² = 1 acre	=	.4 hectacres
1 ounce	=	28 grams
16 oz. = 1 pound	=	.45 kilo (kg.)
1 teaspoon	=	5 milliliters
3 tsp. = 1 tablespoon	=	15 milliliters
2 tbsp. = 1 fluid ounce	=	30 milliliters
8 oz. = 1 cup	=	.24 liters
2 c. = 1 pint	=	.47 liters
2 pt. = 1 quart	=	.95 liters
4 qt. = 1 gallon	=	3.8 liters

Fahrenheit/Centigrade

Conversion formulas:

$$°F - 32 \times 5 \div 9 = °C$$
$$°C \times 9 \div 5 + 32 = °F$$

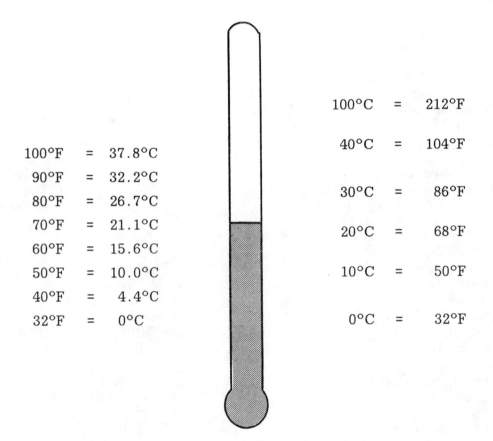

100°F	=	37.8°C
90°F	=	32.2°C
80°F	=	26.7°C
70°F	=	21.1°C
60°F	=	15.6°C
50°F	=	10.0°C
40°F	=	4.4°C
32°F	=	0°C

100°C	=	212°F
40°C	=	104°F
30°C	=	86°F
20°C	=	68°F
10°C	=	50°F
0°C	=	32°F

List #9: Common Symbols

♂	male	$	dollar
♀	female	¢	cent
		£	pound (£3)
		/, s	shilling (5/ or 5s)
+	plus	d	penny, pence (6d)
-	minus		
x	times	~	tilde (cañon)
÷	divided by	^	circumflex (fête)
=	equals	˛	cedilla (Français)
>	greater than	´	acute accent (passé)
<	less than	`	grave accent
≠	not equal to		(à la carte)
√	square root	¨	dieresis (zoölogy)
π	pi	©	copyright
∞	infinity	&	ampersand (and)
		*	asterisk for note
		*	A hypothetical or
°	degree (60°)		wrong form
'	minute (60° 30')		(He *drinked)
"	second (60° 30' 15")		
@	at (@ 80¢ per quart)		
@	approximately		
O/A	on or about		
%	percent		
#	number (#10 nail)		
#	pounds (80#)		
'	foot (6')		
"	inches (6' 2")		
x	by (2' x 4')		

List #10: Common Elements*

Atomic No.	Symbol	Name
1	H	hydrogen
2	He	helium
3	Li	lithium
4	Be	beryllium
5	B	boron
6	C	carbon
7	N	nitrogen
8	O	oxygen
9	F	fluorine
10	Ne	neon
11	Na	sodium
12	Mg	magnesium
13	Al	aluminum
14	Si	silicon
15	P	phosphorous
16	S	sulfur
17	Cl	chlorine
18	Ar	argon
19	K	potassium
20	Ca	calcium
24	Cr	chromium
25	Mn	manganese
26	Fe	iron
27	Co	cobalt
28	Ni	nickel
29	Cu	copper
30	Zn	zinc
33	As	arsenic
47	Ag	silver
50	Sn	tin
51	Sb	antimony
53	I	iodine
56	Ba	barium
78	Pt	platinum
79	Au	gold
80	Hg	mercury
82	Pb	lead
83	Bi	bismuth
88	Ra	radium
92	U	uranium
94	Pu	plutonium

*This list contains only the commonly known elements.

List #11: Abbreviations (abbr., abbrev.)

A.   General (Gen.)

A.A.	Associate of Arts
A.D.	anno Domini, in the year of Our Lord
a.m.	ante meridiem, 'before noon'
Amer.	America
anon.	anonymous
assn.	association
b.	born
B.A., A.B.	Bachelor of Arts
B.C.	before Christ
B.S.	Bachelor of Science
bibliog.	bibliography
biog.	biography
©	copyright
c., ca.	circa 'about'
cf.	confer 'compare'
ch., chap.	chapter
d.	died
D.D.S.	Doctor of Dental Science (Surgery)
dept.	department
E., Eng.	English
ed.	editor, edited by
e.g.	exempli gratia, 'for example'
E.F.L.	English as a foreign language
E.S.L.	English as a second language
E.S.O.L.	English to Speakers of other languages
esp.	especially
ESP	extrasensory perception
E.S.P.	English for special purposes
et al	et alii 'and others'
etc.	et cetera 'and so forth'
ex.	example
f., ff.	and the following page(s)
Fr.	French
Gr.	German
Gk.	Greek
hist.	history
ibid.	ibidem 'in the same place'
i.e.	id est 'that is'
intro.	introduction
It.	Italian

Jr.	junior
lang.	language
L., Lat.	Latin
L.C.	Library of Congress
M.A.	Master of Arts
M.B.A.	Master of Business Administration
M.D.	Doctor of Medicine
misc.	miscellaneous
Miss	Miss
Mr.	Mister
Mrs.	Mistress
Ms.	Woman
ms.	manuscript
M.S.	Master of Science
N.B.	nota bone 'take note, note well'
no.	number
p., pp.	page(s)
par.	paragraph
Ph.D.	Doctor of Philosophy
philos.	philosophy
p.m.	post meridiem 'afternoon'
pub.	published by
q.v.	quod vide 'which see'
rpm	revolutions per minute
Sr.	senior
sic	thus
SOS	help!
Sp.	Spanish
sp.	spelling
St.	Saint
st.	street
T.M.	trademark
univ., U.	university
vol.	volume

B. Days and Months (Mos.)

Jan.	January	Mon.	Monday
Feb.	February	Tue.	Tuesday
Mar., March	March	Wed.	Wednesday
Apr., April	April	Thurs.	Thursday
May	May	Fri.	Friday
June	June	Sat.	Saturday
July	July	Sun.	Sunday
Aug.	August		
Sept.	September		
Oct.	October		
Nov.	November		
Dec.	December		

C. Measures

in.	inch	mm.	millimeter
ft.	foot	cm.	centimeter
yd.	yard	m.	meter
mi.	mile	km.	kilometer
gr.	Eng. gram	g.	metric gram
oz.	ounce	kg.	kilo or kilogram
fl. oz.	fluid ounce	t.	tonnes
lb.	pound		
		ml.	milliliter
tsp.	teaspoon	l.	liter
tbsp.	tablespoon		
c.	cup		
pt.	pint		
qt.	quart		
gal.	gallon		

D. Postal Abbrs.

United States	U.S.
of America	U.S.A.

	Old	New
Alabama	Ala.	AL
Alaska	Alas.	AK
Arizona	Ariz.	AZ
Arkansas	Ark.	AR
California	Calif.	CA
Colorado	Colo.	CO
Connecticut	Conn.	CT
Delaware	Del.	DE
Florida	Fla.	FL

Georgia	Ga.	GA
Hawaii	Ha.	HI
Idaho	Ida.	ID
Illinois	Ill.	IL
Indiana	Ind.	IN
Iowa	Ia.	IA
Kansas	Kan.	KS
Kentucky	Ky.	KY
Louisiana	La.	LA
Maine	Me.	ME
Maryland	Md.	MD
Massachusetts	Mass.	MA
Michigan	Mich.	MI
Minnesota	Minn.	MN
Mississippi	Miss.	MS
Missouri	Mo.	MO
Montana	Mont.	MT
Nebraska	Neb.	NE
Nevada	Nev.	NV
New Hampshire	N.H.	NH
New Jersey	N.J.	NJ
New Mexico	N.M.	NM
New York	N.Y.	NY
North Carolina	N.C.	NC
North Dakota	N.D.	ND
Ohio	Ohio	OH
Oklahoma	Okla.	OK
Oregon	Ore.	OR
Pennsylvania	Penn.	PA
Rhode Island	R.I.	RI
South Carolina	S.C.	SC
South Dakota	S.D.	SD
Tennessee	Tenn.	TN
Texas	Tex.	TX
Utah	Utah	UT
Vermont	Vt.	VT
Virginia	Va.	VA
Washington	Wash.	WA
West Virginia	W.V.	WV
Wisconsin	Wisc.	WI
Wyoming	Wyo.	WY
District of Columbia	D.C.	DC
Puerto Rico	P.R.	PR
Guam	Guam	GU
Virgin Islands	V.I.	VI

Other postal abbrs.

APO	Army Post Office
Blvd.	Boulevard
Byp.	Bypass
Cswy.	Causeway
Ctr.	Center
Cir.	Circle
Ct.	Court
Cres.	Crescent
Dr.	Drive
Expy.	Expressway
Ext.	Extension
Fwy.	Freeway
Gdns.	Gardens
Hts.	Heights
Hwy.	Highway
Jct.	Junction
Ln.	Lane
Pl.	Place
Pt.	Point
Rd.	Road
RFD	Rural Free Delivery
Sq.	Square
St.	Street
Ter.	Terrace
Tpke	Turnpike

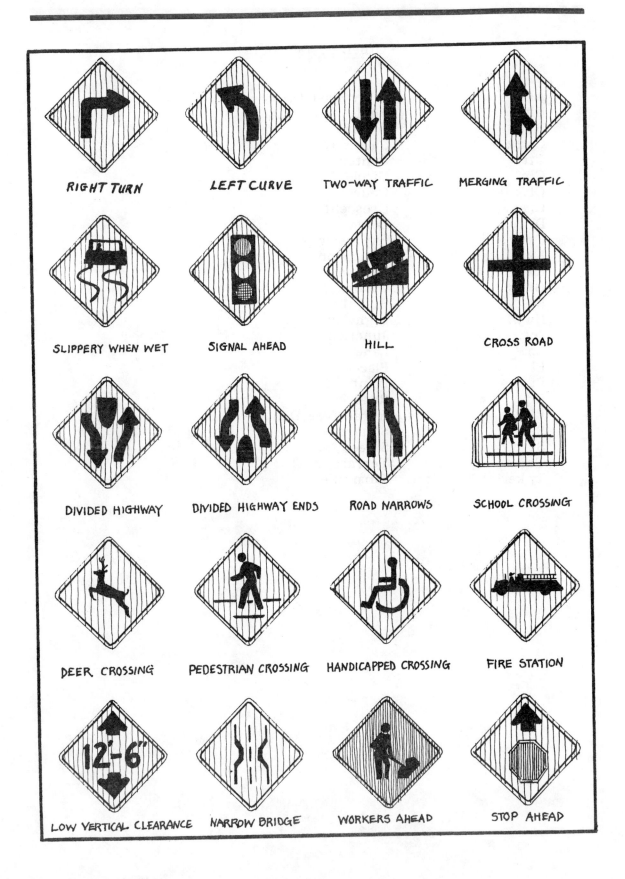

STOP

YIELD

DO NOT ENTER

RAILROAD
ADVANCE CROSSING

NO LEFT TURN

NO RIGHT TURN

NO U TURN

NO PARKING

KEEP LEFT

KEEP RIGHT

LEFT ONLY

RIGHT ONLY

TOW AWAY ZONE

TRUCK WEIGHT LIMIT

SPEED LIMIT

HIKING TRAIL

FOOD

GAS

HOSPITAL

REST AREA

List #13:   Roman Numerals

I, i	1	VI	6	XX	20	CD	400
II, ii	2	VII	7	XL	40	D	500
III, iii	3	VIII	8	L	50	CM	900
IV, iv	4	IX	9	XC	90	M	1000
V, v	5	X	10	C	100		

MCMLXXXI = 1981

List #14:   Proofreading/Correction Marks

∧   insert _a word_ here

⩘   insert comma

⊙   insert period⊙

_e_   delete this

⊂   close up (foot ball)

⑭   paragraph

No ⑭   no paragraph

∿   transpose (their)

insert # space

.....   let it stand

☰   capitalize (washington)

/   lower case (Capital)

Awk.   awkward construction

Frag.   sentence fragment

_Sp._   spelling error

```
┌─────────────────────────────────┐
│  ┌───────────────────────────┐  │
│  │                           │  │
│  │           THE             │  │
│  │                           │  │
│  │     PARALINGUISTIC        │  │
│  │                           │  │
│  │         ASPECT            │  │
│  │                           │  │
│  └───────────────────────────┘  │
└─────────────────────────────────┘
```

We are using the term paralinguistic to include a variety of acts that accompany language or are used in place of language to communicate a message. Sometimes sound itself is used, e.g. a "wolf whistle;" sometimes the body is used, e.g. a smile. In short, this Aspect is about non-verbal communication, but let us hasten to say that it is not about all kinds of non-verbal communication. Painting and sculpture, for example, could be considered non-verbal forms of communication, but because they are only very distant cousins of language, they are not of primary interest to the language learner and teacher, and so we have not dealt with the entire spectrum of non-verbal communication in this Aspect.

Paralinguistic communication does not easily lend itself to a book such as this one. Paralinguistic events such as whistling and smiling are not easily classified and catalogued, as are nouns and verbs, and so we have chosen to present only three examples of paralinguistic communication: the International Sign Alphabet, Classroom Gestures and American Gestures. We have, however, outlined the field of paralinguistics and non-verbal communication. We have included this outline/checklist as a reminder that at some point in the language program it would be useful to discuss and explore the various sounds and actions suggested by the list.

The International Sign Language Alphabet has been included because we feel it is of potential value to language teachers and learners. For example, it can be used in the classroom in instances where a teacher might want to avoid oral spelling. The signs for the vowels might be especially useful because of the discrepancy between the sounds and the names of English vowels (A, E and I give students a lot of trouble). And in general, a sign alphabet might be a useful tool to teachers who try to keep their own verbalizations at a minimum.

The Classroom Gestures are included here only to suggest that there can be a pedagogical use for paralingustic gestures. To a certain extent, such gestures are idiosyncratic, but our brief page of sketches is, we hope, illustrative of some rather widely used classroom gestures. We would like to suggest that teachers and students might be well advised to establish their own system of classroom gestures at the outset of the language program. Our illustrations can be used as a starting point.

The catalog of selected American Gestures speaks for itself. These gestures have been collected, labeled and described by Peg Clement in her thesis A Handful of English: A Photographic Inventory of Typical American Gestures. We have followed her classification system with a few minor changes and we have used her titles, but we have purposefully not included the explanatory text that accompanies each photograph in her collection, or her suggestions for ESL classroom application. In keeping with the style of The ESL Miscellany, we have tried to "just stick to the facts" and let you, teachers and students decide how to deal with the facts.

List #1:   An Outline of Paralinguistic Communication

A.   Sounds

___   1.   Individual Sounds
       a.   Fricatives -- Shh!
       b.   Nasals -- Mmmm.
       c.   Trills -- Brrrr.
       d.   Clicks and stops -- Tsk, tsk; Pst.

___   2.   Emotional Intonation.

       a.   Surprise
       b.   Fear
       c.   Anger
       d.   Sarcasm
       e.   Mockery
       f.   Complaint
       g.   Persuasion
       h.   Flirtation
       i.   Intimacy
       j.   Pleasure

___   3.   Exclamations and Interjections.

___   4.   Voice qualities and styles.

       a.   Whisper
       b.   Baby talk
       c.   falsetto

___   5.   Whistling.
___   6.   Humming.
___   7.   Yelling.
___   8.   Laughing.
___   9.   Crying.
___ 10.   Coughing and throat clearing.

B.   Body Language (Kinesics)

___   1.   Facial expressions.
___   2.   Eye Contact.
___   3.   Gestures
___   4.   Touching (Haptics).

C.   Other Areas of Paralinguistic Communication

___   1.   Silence
___   2.   Time.
___   3.   Space and Distance (Proxemics)

List #2:   International Sign Alphabet

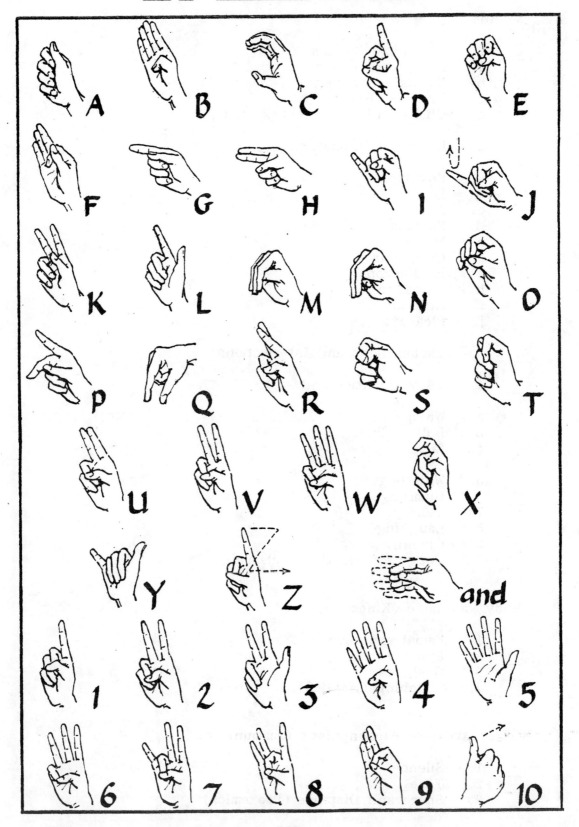

List #3:   Classroom Gestures

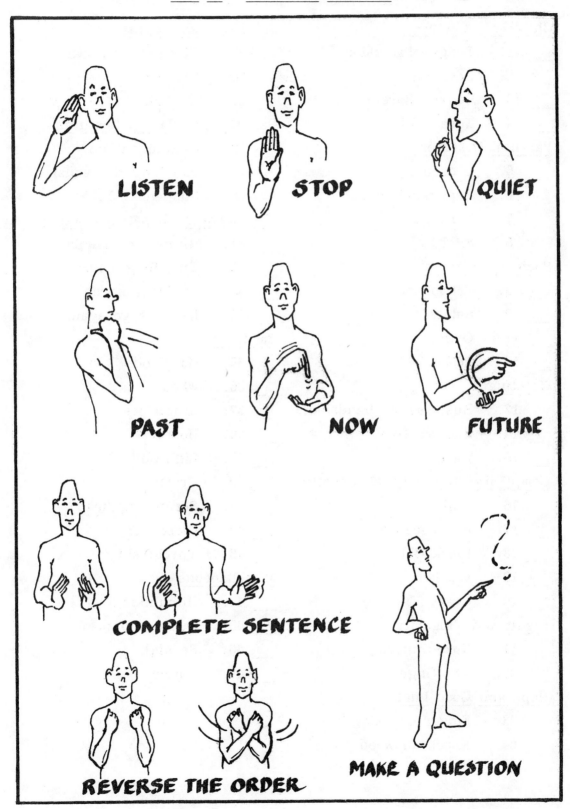

List #4: Checklist of Selected American Gestures

Children's Gestures

___ 1. Tongue Protusion

___ 2. Devil

___ 3. Donkey Ears

___ 4. Nose Holding

Parental Gestures

___ 5. Beckoning

___ 6. Reprimanding

___ 7. Tsk, tsk

___ 8. Shhh.

Societal Gestures

___ 9. Patriotism

___ 10. Salute

___ 11. Oath

___ 12. Peace

Greetings

___ 13. Businessman handshake

___ 14. Slap me five

___ 15. Wave

Complicity, Duplicity, Fraternity

___ 16. Wink

___ 17. Get a load of...

___ 18. Black fist

___ 19. Rib jab

___ 20. Crazy

Insult and Vulgarity

___ 21. Nose-thumbing

___ 23. The finger

Hope and Good Luck

___ 23. Finger Crossing

___ 24. Knock on Wood

Jubilation and Approval

___ 25. Thumbs Up/Down

___ 26. Victory

___ 27. A - Ok

Self Congratulatory Gestures

___ 28. Chalking it up

___ 29. Polishing the medal

___ 30. Suspender hook

Nervousness, Impatience and Boredom

___ 31. Biting fingernails

___ 32. Twiddling Thumbs

___ 33. Shoulder shrug

___ 34. Here we go again

Emotions

___ 35. Mm Good

___ 36. Whoa

___ 37. Stupid me

___ 38. Horrors

___ 39. Lightbulb

___ 40. Crafty

___ 41. Scratching head

___ 42. Close call

___ 43. Throat slit

Miscellaneous

___ 44. Hitchhiking

___ 45. Quote-unquote

___ 46. So high

___ 47. Waiter

2.   Devil

1.   Tongue Protusion

3.   Donkey Ears

4.   Nose Holding

5.   Beckoning

6.   Reprimanding

7.   Tsk Tsk

8.   Shhh

9.   Patriotism   10   Salute

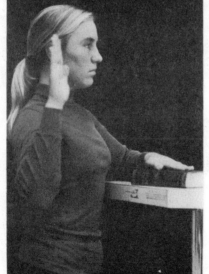

11.   Oath   12.   Peace

13.   Businessman Handshake

14.   Slap Me Five

15.   Wave

16. Wink

17. Get a Load of...

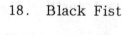

18. Black Fist

19. Rib Jab

20. Crazy

21. Nose-Thumbing

22. Finger

HOPE AND GOOD LUCK

23. Finger Crossing

24. Knock on Wood

25. Thumbs Up/Down

26. Victory   27. A-OK

28.   Chalking It Up

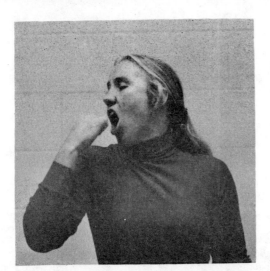

29.   Polishing The Medal

30.   Suspender Thumb Hook

31. Biting Fingernails

32. Twiddling Thumbs

33. Shoulder Shrug

34. Here We Go Again

35. Mm Good

36. Whoa

37. Stupid Me

38. Horrors

39. Lightbulb

40. Crafty

41. Scratching Head

42. Close Call

43. Throat Slit

44. Hitchhiking

45. Quote-Unquote

46. So High

47. Waiter

SOURCES

Boone, Eleanor; Rick Gildea and Pat Moran. Resources for TESOL Teaching (Program and Training Journal 26). Washington D.C.: ACTION/Peace Corps, 1978.

Clement, Margaret. A Handful of Gestures. Unpublished MAT Thesis, School for International Training, 1978.

Marcella, Frank. Modern English: A Practical Reference Guide. Englewood Cliffs, N.J.: Prentice-Hall, 1972.

Guntermann, Gail. "Purposeful Communication Practice: Developing Functional Proficiency in a Foreign Language." FL Annals (XII, No. 3), 1979.

The Hammond Almanac. Maplewood, N.J.: Hammond Almanac, Inc., 1981.

Hayden, Rebecca E; Dorothy Pilgrim and Aurora Quiros Haggard. Mastering American English. Englewood Cliffs, N.J.: Prentice-Hall, 1956.

Key, Mary Ritchie. Paralanguage and Kinesics. Metuchen, N.J.: The Scarecrow Press, 1975.

Kin, David. ed. Dictionary of American Proverbs. New York: Philosophical Library.

Krohn, Robert et al. English Sentence Structure. Ann Arbor: University of Michigan Press, 1971.

Mencken, H.L. The American Language, Fourth Edition. New York: Alfred E. Knopf, 1936.

Murdock, George P. "The Common Denominators of Culture" in The Science of Man in the World Crisis, Ralph Linton, ed. New York: Columbia University Press, 1945.

Parnell, E.C. Oxford Picture Dictionary of American English. New York: Oxford University Press, 1978.

Praninskas, Jean. Rapid Review of English Grammar (2nd edition). Englewood Cliffs, N.J.: Prentice-Hall, 1975.

Quirk, Randolph. A Concise Grammar of Contemporary English. New York: Harcourt, Brace, 1973.

Radford, E and M.A.   Encyclopaedia of Superstitions.   New York: Philosophical Library, 1949.

Rutherford, William E.   Modern English.   New York: Harcourt, Brace and World, 1968.

Silber, Irwin and Fred.   The Folksingers Wordbook.   New York: Oak Publications, 1973.

Wallechinsky, David, and Irving Wallace.   The People's Almanac. Garden City, N.J.: Doubleday & Company, Inc., 1975.

Wilkins, D.A.   Notional Syllabuses.   Oxford: Oxford University Press, 1976.

Whitford, Harold C. and Robert J. Dixson.   Handbook of American Idioms and Idiomatic Usage. New York: Regents, 1953.

The World Almanac.   New York: Newspaper Enterprise Association, Inc., 1980.

INDEX

PRO LINGUA ASSOCIATES

We, **Pro Lingua Associates**, have a distinctive approach to language learning and teaching which we call the **Interplay** approach. All of the materials we publish are chosen because they support the efforts of teachers taking our approach. Ray Clark has written an essay explaining our ideas, and it is given as an appendix to our basic how-to book, **Language Teaching Techniques.** Stated simply,

Interplay invites language learners and teachers to

interact with the materials, with the language and

the culture, and with each other in active, creative,

and productive play.

Our books are published in three series, **Teacher's Resource Handbooks, Supplementary Materials Handbooks,** and our series of student texts titled, **Interplay ESL.** We are actively developing each of these series, so if you would like a copy of our latest catalogue explaining all of our most recent titles, please write to us. We would also appreciate some interplay with you, teachers and students using our books, and we encourage you to send us comments and suggestions.

TEACHER'S RESOURCE HANDBOOKS

Language Teaching Techniques: 26 basic techniques, 13 designed to improve communicative skills and 13 to improve grammatical accuracy. They are presented in a clear, illustrated format. **$6.50**

The ESL Miscellany

Experiential Language Teaching Techniques: 28 carefully structured out-of-class activities for learning the language and culture of the United States. Step-by-step directions for student preparation and enjoyable, revealing follow-up activites. **$9.50**

SUPPLEMENTARY MATERIALS HANDBOOKS

Index Card Games for ESL: Clearly explained and easy to play games providing practice in pronunciation and spelling, vocabulary building, questioning, sentence structure, conversation, and playing with and in English. Games are useful pace breakers. **$6.00**

Lexicarry: An illustrated vocabulary builder for students at anly level studying any language. The "game element" engages students actively and imaginatively and stimulates their memories. An English Word List is included; word lists in other languages are available. **$5.75**

INTERPLAY ESL

The Grammar Handbook, Part One: 52 basic English grammar points are explained very simply, classroom activities are outlined and open worksheets, either blank or illustrated, are provided for them, and references are given for both the teacher and student. **$6.00**

Smalltown Daily: 288 authentic news articles are presented in newspaper format. There are 24 for each month, 96 at each reading proficiency level. A compelling study of American culture from the perspective of a real American smalltown daily newspaper. **$7.50**

Orders, prepaid with shipping (10%/$1.00 min.), to **PRO LINGUA ASSOCIATES,** 15 Elm Street, Brattleboro, Vermont 05301. Telephone 802 257 7779.